FAMOUS IMMIGRANT
ARTISTS

MAKING AMERICA GREAT
IMMIGRANT SUCCESS STORIES

FAMOUS IMMIGRANT
ARTISTS

Adam Furgang

E **Enslow Publishing**
101 W. 23rd Street
Suite 240
New York, NY 10011
USA
enslow.com

Published in 2018 by Enslow Publishing, LLC.
101 W. 23rd Street, Suite 240, New York, NY 10011

Library of Congress Cataloging-in-Publication Data

Names: Furgang, Adam, author.
Title: Famous immigrant artists / Adam Furgang.
Description: New York : Enslow, 2018. | Series: Making America great : immigrant success stories | Includes bibliographical references and index. | Audience: Grades 7 to 12.
Identifiers: LCCN 2017015083 | ISBN 9780766092457 (library bound) | ISBN 9780766095915 (paperback)
Subjects: LCSH: Artists—United States—Biography—Juvenile literature. | Immigrants—United States—Biography—Juvenile literature.
Classification: LCC NX511.5 .F87 2017 | DDC 700.92/2 [B]—dc23
LC record available at https://lccn.loc.gov/2017015083

Printed in the United States of America

To Our Readers: We have done our best to make sure all websites in this book were active and appropriate when we went to press. However, the author and the publisher have no control over and assume no liability for the material available on those websites or on any websites they may link to. Any comments or suggestions can be sent by email to customerservice@enslow.com.

Photo credits: Cover, p. 3 AFP/Getty Images; cover and interior pages (stars) saicle/Shutterstock. com; pp. 6–7 Stock Montage/Archive Photos/Getty Images; pp. 11, 20–21, 60–61, 63 Bettmann /Getty Images; p. 14 Newark Museum/Art Resource, NY; p. 16 Allan Grant/The LIFE Picture Collection/Getty Images; pp. 18–19 Keystone/Hulton Archive/Getty Images; p. 23 Frank Scherschel/ The LIFE Picture Collection/Getty Images; p. 25 Science & Society Picture Library/Getty Images; p. 27 Pictorial Press Ltd/Alamy Stock Photo; pp. 30–31 Everett Collection Historical/Alamy Stock Photo; p. 32 AT History/Alamy Stock Photo; pp. 34–35 © AP Images; pp. 38–39 Soltan Frédéric/ Sygma/Getty Images; pp. 40–41 Library of Congress/Corbis Historical/Getty Images; p. 43 Photo 12/Alamy Stock Photo; p. 45 Henry Groskinsky/The LIFE Picture Collection/Getty Images; p. 47 hans engbers/Shutterstock.com; p. 49 Smallz & Raskind/Getty Images; pp. 52–53 Andrew Toth /Getty Images; pp. 56-57 Mirrorpix/Getty Images; p. 67 Bill Watters/Getty Images; p. 69 ullstein bild /Getty Images; pp. 70–71 Chris Hondros/Getty Images; pp. 74–75 Charley Gallay/Getty Images; pp. 76–77 Moviestore collection Ltd/Alamy Stock Photo; p. 81 AF archive/Alamy Stock Photo; pp. 84–85 Lee Jaffe/Hulton Archive/Getty Images; p. 86 Jemal Countess/WireImage/Getty Images; p. 88 Jim Dyson/Getty Images; p. 90 Johnny Nunez/WireImage/Getty Images; p. 92 John Moore /Getty Images.

Contents

INTRODUCTION 6

CHAPTER 1
PAINTERS 10

CHAPTER 2
PHOTOGRAPHERS 25

CHAPTER 3
SCULPTORS 37

CHAPTER 4
MIXED MEDIA ARTISTS 51

CHAPTER 5
COMIC BOOK ARTISTS 62

CHAPTER 6
FILM AND ANIMATION ARTISTS 73

CHAPTER 7
STREET ARTISTS 83

CHAPTER NOTES 94
GLOSSARY 104
FURTHER READING 106
INDEX 109
ABOUT THE AUTHOR 112

Introduction

Art has been described as a universal language because people from different cultures, countries, and time periods have always enjoyed it. Throughout history, human beings have created art as they moved from place to place around the globe. These immigrants, like others, have traveled to the United States for a number of reasons. War, hunger, poverty, education, religious freedom, and hope for a better life cause people to move away, or emigrate, from their countries of birth.

For centuries, immigrants have come to North and South America. Long before Europeans such as Christopher Columbus arrived in the late 1400s, however, Native Americans lived there. Their ancestors were the first people to settle in North America, which they'd made their home thousands of years before Columbus's arrival. According to a 2012 research study from Harvard University, Native Americans likely first came to North America from Asia around fifteen thousand years ago. They might have made the trip by way of the Bering Strait, the land bridge thought to have once connected the continents of Asia and North America. Scientists believe that during the last ice age, when sea levels were lower and more land was exposed, humans were able to cross the continents and fill the Americas with their children, grandchildren, and so on.

This illustration from 1754 shows a Native American village of longhouses. Before Dutch colonists arrived from Europe, Native Americans were living in what is now Manhattan, New York. The colonists arrived in the 16th or early 17th century.

In 2017, a group of scientists questioned the Bering Strait theory. They said ancient mastodon bones found in San Diego County, California, show that humans lived in North America 130,000 years ago. Tests performed on these prehistoric bones have led researchers to believe that humans used tools to break them apart. If true, humans have lived in North America far longer than researchers have believed, and the many Native Americans who disagree with the Bering Strait theory will now have science on their side. Whenever humans settled in the Americas, they made art such as pottery and rock carvings upon their arrival, leaving their mark on the world.

After Columbus's arrival in 1492, large numbers of Europeans came to North America. Columbus landed on an island that is now part of the Bahamas. In the 1500s, Spain, France, England, and other European nations sent their citizens to North America. The places where these Europeans lived became colonies that led to the creation of the United States after the American Revolution of the 1770s.

By the mid 1800s, the American population topped more than 23 million people,[1] including 2.2 million immigrants.[2] By 2014, the United States had grown to nearly 320 million people,[3] including 42.2 million[4] immigrants. That's a whopping 13.2 percent of the nation's population.

Immigrants have given much to the country. Artists, for example, contribute to the culture and enjoyment of citizens. This book will discuss the achievements of the most famous immigrant artists who've come to the United States of America. Unknown immigrant artists also contribute to American life and make it better with their creativity; they just haven't received as much attention for their work.

As a group, foreign-born artists living in America have made new styles of art popular. Some became great artists in the United States, while others were already well known before arriving in their new country. Immigrants have also influenced American-born artists, many of whom have parents and grandparents who came to the United States from faraway lands. Their ancestors may have arrived on New York City's Ellis Island before starting their new lives in the United States to chase the American dream.

Both now and then, immigrants living in the United States have contributed not just to the world of art, but to every part of life that makes America great.

CHAPTER 1

PAINTERS

Immigrants have taken part in the wide variety of painting styles that have developed in the United States. Immigrant painters have made a major impact on the modern art movements known as Futurism, Dada, Cubism, and Surrealism. Such painters include John James Audubon, Joseph Stella, Marcel Duchamp, and Max Ernst.

JOHN JAMES AUDUBON

John James Audubon was a naturalist painter, meaning he portrayed scenes from nature in his work. He became famous for his paintings of North American birds. He also worked as an ornithologist—a person who studies birds and their behavior.

He was born on April 26, 1785, in Les Cayes, Saint Domingue, now known as Haiti. His parents were French plantation owner Captain Jean Audubon and his Creole (biracial) servant Jeanne Rabin.

Audubon received the name Jean Rabin at birth, but his mother died soon afterward. His father then moved Jean and his sister to Nantes, France. There, his father's wife, Anne, legally adopted him in 1794, and he received the new name Jean Jacques Fougére Audubon.

John James Audubon painted this self-portrait using oil paint. He created the painting at Beech Woods, Feliciana Parish, Louisiana, in 1822. He was thirty-seven at the time.

Once adopted, Jean received an education in the arts, nature, and music. He also had a lot of free time as a child, which sparked his interest in nature. He became fond of birds and drew pictures of them throughout his youth.

In 1803, when Audubon was eighteen, war began between France and Britain. His father did not want him to serve in Napoleon's army, so he sent him to a farm he owned in Mill Grove, Pennsylvania.

Audubon entered the United States with a fake passport, making him an undocumented immigrant. This means he lacked the paperwork and permission needed to enter the country legally. At some point, he changed his name to John James Audubon and became an American citizen in 1812.[1]

In the United States, he continued his studies of birds and the natural world. In 1808, he married Lucy Bakewell. The couple moved to Kentucky, where they had two sons, Victor Gifford and John Woodhouse. While in Kentucky, Audubon ran a dry goods store, a business that sold clothes, threads, and other items. He suffered from financial problems, and in 1819, he spent time in jail because he did not pay his bills.

In 1820, Audubon moved his family to New Orleans, Louisiana. His wife earned money as a governess, which is a private, in-home teacher. During this time, Audubon painted and sold portraits, taught drawing, and painted and studied birds. By 1824, he'd finished so many paintings of birds that he tried to find someone to publish them in a book. Finding no publishers in the United States, he left for England two years later. He displayed his images in Scotland and England, receiving much praise.

In 1827, he found a book publisher, Havell & Son, for his artwork. His four-volume book, *Birds of America,* was in print until 1838. Another book, *Ornithological Biography,* followed and featured Audubon's many experiences as well as bird species behaviors and habits. Another of his books, *A Synopsis of the Birds of North America,* came out in 1839.

After his success, Audubon moved to Manhattan in New York City, where he continued painting. In 1843, his work focused on mammals rather than birds, but he could no longer see well. Audubon died on January 27, 1851. He is considered one of the most important naturalists of his time, and his love and appreciation of nature has inspired people to protect bird species around the world. The National Audubon Society, which started in 1886, was named in his honor, as were many parks and wildlife sanctuaries around the country.

JOSEPH STELLA

Joseph Stella was a Futurist painter. These painters focused on movement, technology, and speed in their artwork. Stella, in particular, became famous for his paintings of New York City and the Brooklyn Bridge.

He was born Giuseppe Michele Stella in the village of Muro Lucano, Italy, on June 13, 1877. As a child, Giuseppe loved drawing and art. He was also a good student who did well in his English and French classes. In 1896, at the age of nineteen, he immigrated to the United States. When his family reached Ellis Island, he received a new Americanized name, Joseph Stella.

At first, Stella planned to study medicine like his doctor brother, but he changed his mind two years later. A class he had taken at the Art Students League motivated him to transfer to the New York School of Art.[2]

Artist Robert Henri encouraged Stella to focus on New York City's immigrants for inspiration in his work. Stella's art about immigrants helped to spread the idea that immigrants should be treated fairly. It also brought attention to the challenges they faced.[3]

Stella went on to work as a magazine illustrator from 1905 to 1909. He also began to concentrate on painting, and in 1906, the

Joseph Stella painted the Brooklyn Bridge several times throughout his life. He completed this work, *The Voice of the City of New York Interpreted: The Bridge*, from 1920 to 1922. He used oil on canvas and tempera on canvas as mediums.

Society of American Artists in New York showed his painting *The Old Man*. His illustrations of American immigrants and miners appeared in the magazines the *Outlook* and the *Survey*. Illustrations he produced of a mining disaster in Monongah, West Virginia, made more people aware of the event and helped to create better safety laws for miners.

Stella traveled back to Europe in 1909 and stayed in Italy for a year. He visited the Italian cities of Florence, Naples, and Rome and returned to his home village, Muro Lucano. When he later visited Paris, he found out about Italian Futurist painters Umberto Boccioni, Carlo Carra, and Gino Severini. The Futurist style stood out for its vivid colors and portrayals of modern machines.

Stella's Futurist paintings *Battle of Lights*, *Coney Island*, and *Mardi Gras* were some of the first he did after returning to the United States. He displayed some of his work in the 1913 New York Armory show and focused on the Brooklyn Bridge as a subject because it related to the Futurist themes of modern inventions and technology. Stella's 1919 painting *Brooklyn Bridge* is one of his most memorable paintings.

During the 1920s, Stella's popularity grew, and he began to explore architecture in New York City. Stella became an American citizen in 1923 but made many trips back to Europe between 1926 and 1934. Over time, his painting styles and subject matter changed.

In 1934, Stella moved to the Bronx with his wife, Mary. He then became involved with the WPA, or Works Progress Administration. The government-run program helped artists earn money during the Great Depression, when the nation's economy was in serious trouble. He continued to work for the WPA until 1937.

In the 1940s, Stella's health began to suffer, and doctors diagnosed him with heart disease. He died from heart failure in 1946. Joseph Stella's paintings had a huge impact on many other

Marcel Duchamp sits behind one of his famous accidentally cracked glass Dada artworks. He created this piece, *To Be Looked at (from the Other Side of the Glass) with One Eye, Close to, for Almost an Hour*, in 1918.

artists, and his Futurist paintings are considered excellent examples of American art.

MARCEL DUCHAMP

Marcel Duchamp was born July 28, 1887, in Blainville, France. His parents, Eugene and Lucie Duchamp, had six children. His father was a notary, a person who witnesses the signing of important papers and takes sworn statements from the public, among other duties. Eugene became mayor of Blainville in 1895, while his wife, who liked painting, raised the children. Four of the six Duchamp children studied art and became well-known artists, although Marcel was by far the most famous.

When Marcel was eight, he followed his older brothers Jacques and Raymond to study at an excellent school called Lycée Pierre-Corneille in Rouen, France. Marcel spent eight years there, getting high marks in math and art. In 1904, he moved to Paris to study painting at the private art school Académie Julian. In addition to receiving financial support from his brother Jacques, he earned money from drawing cartoons.[4]

Duchamp's work revealed his interest in several art movements of the late 1800s and early 1900s, including Impressionism, Fauvism, and Cubism. He painted one of his most famous works, *Nude Descending a Staircase, No. 2*, in 1912. The painting shows a naked woman walking down a staircase. He received both praise and criticism for the piece. Then at age twenty-five, possibly because of the controversy about his nude, he stopped painting.

For his later artwork, Duchamp used everyday objects that he called "readymades." According to the Museum of Modern Art's website, he said, "An ordinary object [could be] elevated to the dignity of a work of art by the mere choice of an artist."[5] In 1913, he chose a bicycle wheel as one of his first readymade pieces.

WAR AND IMMIGRATION

Wars around the world lead to immigration because people in the areas affected leave to escape the dangers of life in a battle zone. World War II in particular caused many important artists in Europe to leave their homes. On June 14, 1940, Germany invaded Paris, then the center of the art world.

Marcel Duchamp, Yves Tanguy, Max Ernst, Marc Chagall, Salvador Dali, and Piet Mondrian are some of the many artists who immigrated to New York City after the invasion. Although many European artists returned home after the war, during their time in the United States they taught American painters about modern art styles such as Surrealism, Dada, and Cubism. This caused the center of the art world to shift from Paris to New York.

This July 1943 bombing left Hamburg, Germany partially destroyed. World War II made an impact on immigration around the world. It not only caused the emigration of artists, but it also put important artwork at risk.

In 1915, after the beginning of World War I, Duchamp immigrated to New York. He then spent seven years working on a large metal and glass piece, *The Bride Stripped Bare by Her Bachelors, Even*. It is often called *The Large Glass* (1915–1923) as well. Duchamp put much time and energy into the piece, making many diagrams, drawings, tests, and sketches for it. He gathered these papers together for his work, *The Green Box* (1934), which explained the purpose of *The Large Glass*. Years later, as *The Large Glass* was being moved, the piece became damaged and many cracks spread throughout it.[6] Duchamp did not mind this change and felt that it completed the work in a way that he never could have.

In 1923, Duchamp returned to Paris and worked with other artists, but nineteen years later, he came back to the United States and teamed up with the famous artist Joseph Cornell. The two spent much time together, and Cornell kept a box called The Duchamp Dossier (1942–1953) containing many mementos from this period. The public did not learn about this piece until Cornell's death in 1972.

Duchamp did not become a United States citizen until 1955. Later in life, he moved to Neuilly-sur-Seine, France, and stayed there until he died on October 2, 1968. Duchamp's paintings and artwork continued to inspire artists around the world.

MAX ERNST

Maximilian Maria Ernst was born on April 2, 1891, in Brühl, Germany. He lived in a large family of nine children. His only training in art came from his father, Philip, who was not a professional painter. In 1914, Ernst studied philosophy at the University of Bonn but soon dropped out and devoted himself to art.

Surrealist painter Max Ernst stands in front of his painting, *The Temptation of St. Anthony.* He created the painting in 1945. A variety of other artists painted versions as well.

Ernst never received formal training. Early in his career, he enjoyed the art of Vincent van Gogh, August Macke, and Giorgio de Chirico, whose dreamlike images fascinated him. In 1914, Ernst fought as a soldier in World War I. After the war, he returned home to Cologne in 1918 and married Luise Straus. He then began to collage different pictures together. Although he was not the first artist to do so, he became very well known because of his collages. Ernst used photos, printed catalogues, and animals from science books for his artwork.

THE "IMMIGRANT" ART COLLECTION OF PEGGY GUGGENHEIM

Art collector Peggy Guggenheim came from a wealthy Jewish American family in New York City. After the start of World War II, she gave up her dream to open an art museum in London and instead used her money to buy modern art in Paris. Because of the war, many artists sold their works at cheaper than normal prices. She famously set out to "buy a picture a day" and managed to get fifty works of art in the months before the Germans invaded Paris.[7]

She collected work from artists such as Salvador Dali, Max Ernst, Alberto Giacometti, René Magritte, Man Ray, and Joan Miró.[8] She hid her collection from the Nazis during the war and returned with the art, as well as with Ernst, André Breton, and Breton's family, to New York in July 1941.

Today, Peggy Guggenheim's art collection contains over three hundred works of art and is located in Venice, Italy. She died on December 23, 1979, in Camposampiero, Italy. She is now remembered as one of the most important art collectors of the twentieth century.

Famous American art collector Peggy Guggenheim stands in her dining room at Venier dei Leoni Palace in Venice, Italy in 1953. The large painting on the right is Pablo Picasso's *On the Beach*.

Ernst was a friend of French artist Jean Arp, who helped start the Dada art movement.[9] The movement rebelled against tradition and pride in one's country during a period in which war took so many lives. The Dada movement began in 1916 in a club called the Cabaret Voltaire in Zürich, Switzerland. Ernst and Arp worked together to start a Dada group in Cologne, Germany. One of their art shows revealed how strange Dada was. It took place in a bathroom, and viewers were told to destroy one of Ernst's sculptures with an axe.

In 1922, Ernst moved to Paris without his wife and remained there until 1941. During this time, he took an interest in Surrealism, an art movement that explored the connection between dreams, fantasy, and reality. In his work, Ernst focused on new ways of thinking and used new art techniques to create images. In 1927, Ernst married his second wife, Marie-Berthe Aurenche.

After World War II began in 1941, Ernst, along with André Breton and his family, escaped to the United States with the help of art collector Peggy Guggenheim. Once in New York, Ernst began to influence the local art scene. Ernst and Guggenheim became close, and when the United States entered World War II, Guggenheim insisted that she and Ernst get married. This allowed him to stay in the country legally. The couple wed December 30, 1941,[10] but their marriage lasted only a few years. Ernst did not become an American citizen until 1948.[11]

Ernst then married Dorothea Tanning, a Surrealist, and moved to Sedona, Arizona, in 1946, where they lived until moving to France in 1953. He became a French citizen five years later.[12] Ernst continued to make art until April 1, 1976, when he died in Paris.[13] One of the artists who started Surrealism, his art had a huge impact on the United States and the world.

CHAPTER 2

PHOTOGRAPHERS

Photography has the power to record reality and freeze history in time. Today cell phones and the internet have made photography very common. As many as 1.3 trillion photos will be taken in 2017, according to the *New York Times*. But it was not always so easy to take a picture and share it. Photography is a pretty new art form, invented in 1827 when Joseph Nicéphore Niépce recorded the first permanent photograph on film. It took about eight hours to expose completely to sunlight.[1]

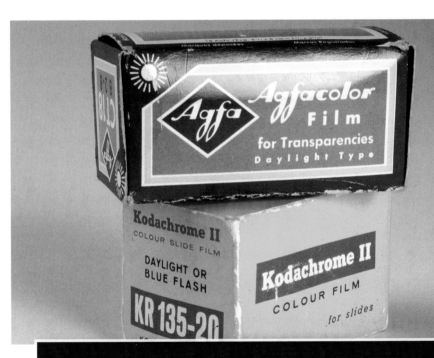

Kodak produced the first color slide film in 1936. Once developed, film like these boxes of Agfacolor and Kodachrome II could be seen through a slide projector.

Eventually the process improved, but the art form still remained out of reach for most people because of its cost and the skill needed to take photographs.

In 1887, plastic rolls of film were invented and used for almost one hundred years.[2] Once digital photography became popular in the 1990s, it quickly replaced film, which is now mostly used by professionals, artists, and people who prefer traditional photography. Today, most photos are taken with cell phone cameras.

Families around the world have recorded their lives with photography, including being an immigrant in a new country. In fact, some of the best-known and most talented photographers have been immigrants, such as Eadweard Muybridge and Elliott Erwitt.

EADWEARD MUYBRIDGE

Eadweard Muybridge was a photographer best known for his motion picture photography. He was one of the first photographers to record the beautiful landscapes of the American West. Remembered as an eccentric, or strange, man with a long white beard, Muybridge was originally named Edward James Muggeridge.[3]

He was born in a town called Kingston upon Thames, England, on April 9, 1830. He grew up with three brothers, and his father, John, ran a barge business along the River Thames. John also sold coal and grain.[4] After his father's death in 1843, Muybridge's mother, Susan, helped to run the business. The telegraph and train rail service both started during Muybridge's youth, and he would later make trains the subject of his photography.

He experienced family loss in his early life. His older brother, John, went away to boarding school but came home after the start of his second year. John soon became sick and died in 1847. Muybridge was only sixteen at the time and had already lost his father.[5]

Three years later, Muybridge immigrated to the United States aboard the steamship *Liverpool*; he arrived in New York on

Eadweard Muybridge's advancements in motion photography changed the way people saw the world. His work paved the way for motion picture photography and animation. Muybridge's photography influenced a number of artists.

July 16, 1850. He moved to San Francisco in 1855 and sold books and printed materials to earn money.[6] He successfully applied for US citizenship in 1856 and changed the spelling of his name.[7]

While traveling to the East Coast before a trip to England in 1860, Muybridge hurt his head badly. He was thrown from a horse-drawn carriage and knocked unconscious. "I awakened nine days after the accident, in Fort Smith, Arkansas," Muybridge remembered afterward. "I had a wound on my head and double vision. I had no

PHOTOGRAPHS OF US IMMIGRANTS

Ellis Island stands out as the most famous place that immigrants arrived in the United States. It is located in New York Harbor. Between 1892 and 1954, more than twelve million immigrants passed through the Island.[8]

From 1892 to 1925, Augustus Frederick Sherman worked as a clerk on Ellis Island. He also took photos of the many immigrants who passed through the national entry point. Although he was not a trained photographer, *National Geographic* magazine published some of his photos in 1907. Sherman's photos could also be found on the walls of the Immigration Service building in New York City.

The New York Public Library, the National Parks Service, the Library of Congress, and the National Archives are just a few places students can visit to explore the many photos that have been taken of people from around the world arriving in the United States.

taste, and my sense of smell was impaired."[9] Although he did not receive good medical care at the time, Muybridge eventually got better. But "friends noticed a marked difference in his behavior," according to Biography.com. "Studies by modern neurologists examining the medical records speculate that the injury to his frontal cortex might have led to some emotional and eccentric behavior later in his life."[10]

After trying to make a living as an inventor, Muybridge became a businessman but did not succeed, so he took up photography and recorded images all over San Francisco, California. At first, most people didn't know about his work, but by 1868 his gorgeous photographs of California's Yosemite Valley brought him much fame.

In 1873, Leland Stanford, one of the founders of the Central Pacific Railroad, asked Muybridge if he could help him with something. Stanford loved horses and figured that all four of a horse's legs would not touch the ground while galloping. He asked Muybridge to use his camera to find out for sure. The artist's photograph of a horse frozen in motion brought him more fame because it had never been done before. Unfortunately, the photo was out of focus, so Stanford's question went unanswered.

In addition to the attention his beautiful photographs gave him, Muybridge made headlines for something quite wicked— murder! In 1871, Muybridge married Flora Downs, but on October 17, 1874, he found letters revealing that she'd cheated on him with a man named Harry Larkyns. So, Muybridge shot and killed Larkyns. At his 1875 trial, Muybridge tried to convince the jury that he was insane but with no luck. The jury did believe, however, that he'd killed for good reason. This is known as justifiable homicide.[11] Because of the jury's decision, Muybridge was freed from prison. He and Downs divorced, and Muybridge moved to Central America for a year to avoid attention from the public and media.

In 1877, Muybridge returned to the United States and continued his motion photography experiments with financial help from Stanford.[12] He photographed horses by using up to twenty-four

In 1879, Eadweard Muybridge used roughly two-dozen cameras to prove through photography that all four hooves leave the ground when horses gallop. His photos of horses made him famous because no photographer had captured a horse in motion.

cameras with equipment that could shoot at a rate of two milliseconds per picture. Doing this allowed everyone to see that, yes, all four of a horse's legs do leave the ground as it gallops.

Muybridge created a motion picture projector called a zoopraxiscope to show motion for the very first time. The device used a rotating disk so the viewer could see the images move quickly in order, giving the impression of motion. At the 1893 Chicago World's Fair, the zoopraxiscope became a popular exhibit.

Between the years of 1884 and 1887 Muybridge continued his photographic research of motion, taking thousands of pictures. In 1887, he put several of his sequences of animals and nudes in motion into a book called *Animal Locomotion: An Electro-Photographic Investigation of Consecutive Phases of Animal Movements*.

In 1895 Muybridge moved home to England and remained there until his death on May 8, 1904. His photography, motion sequence photographs, and the zoopraxiscope led to the invention of motion pictures. Muybridge's important scientific and photographic contributions were the first step in what eventually became a multi-billion dollar industry—the cinema and motion picture industry. He is remembered today as one of the most important photographers in American history and around the world.

Eadweard Muybridge was a photographer and an inventor. He created the motion picture projector known as a zoopraxiscope. The device uses a rotating disk that allows viewers to see a rapid sequence of images, giving the impression of motion.

ELLIOT ERWITT

Elliott Erwitt is known for black-and-white photography that captures the human spirit. His work shows the beauty of cities, and his portraits of celebrities and world figures made them seem just as human as everyone else. His photos also showed the harsh realities of major news stories during the twentieth century as well as the humor and craziness of ordinary life.

Elliot Erwitt was born to Russian Jewish parents in Paris, France, in 1928. He moved with his family to the United States in 1938 when he was ten years old. His name, originally Elio Romano Erwitt, was changed to the more Americanized Elliot at this time.[13] They lived in New York until his parents separated in 1941, and Elliot moved to Los Angeles with his father. At the age of sixteen, Elliot was on his own after his father left him to move to New Orleans. But the teenager continued to go to school. He studied photography and took pictures of weddings to earn money.

At Los Angeles City College, Erwitt learned more about photography. In 1948, he moved to New York City and studied photography and filmmaking at the New School for Social Research. While traveling in Italy and France in 1949, he became a professional photographer. Two years later, Erwitt was drafted into the United States Army and stationed in New Jersey, Germany, and France, where he continued to take pictures—both for the army and professionally.

After his military service ended in 1953, Erwitt joined the Magnum Photos agency at the invitation of famous war photojournalist Robert Capa.[14] The agency, which opened after World War II, was started by four legendary photographers: Henri Cartier-Bresson, Robert Capa, George Rodger, and David Seymour. According to the Magnum Photos website, "Magnum photographers are a rarity and the agency is self-selecting; membership is a minimum four-year process and is considered the finest accolade of a photographer's career."[15] Erwitt was president of Magnum Photos for three terms beginning in 1968.

ICONIC WAR PHOTO: THE TERROR OF WAR

Photography has the power to bring attention to world events, including the horrors of wartime. The Vietnam War photo "The Terror of War," also known as "Napalm Girl," is one such work. Associated Press photographer Nick Ut shot the photo on June 8, 1972, after a napalm attack on a village. Napalm is a jelly made of gasoline and other substances used in bombs.

The "The Terror of War" picture shows a group of children running in fear after the attack. One of them, a young girl named Phan Thị Kim Phúc, is screaming and nude. Napalm badly burned part of her body. Aside from just taking the picture, Ut worked to get the young girl the medical help she needed. She got treatment at an American hospital, which probably saved her life.[16] The United States ended its war with Vietnam in 1973. For his photo, Ut won the Pulitzer Prize, one of the highest honors a photojournalist can receive.

The photographer, born in Long An, Vietnam, is now an American citizen. The little girl in the photo, Phan Thị Kim Phúc, born in Trang Bang, South Vietnam, is now a Canadian citizen.

Nick Ut's photograph *The Terror of War* has become one of the most famous images depicting the horror of war. The photograph has continually generated controversy since it was first taken in 1972.

Throughout his career, he photographed many celebrities and world figures of the 1960s and 1970s, such as President John F. Kennedy, Arnold Schwarzenegger, Che Guevara, and Fidel Castro. He took now famous photos of Marilyn Monroe and Marlon Brando while they worked on the set of their films *The Seven Year Itch and On the Waterfront.*

Photographing dogs became another passion of Erwitt, and in 1979 he published his first book on the subject. He has since gone on to publish three more. Erwitt's dog photos were often humorous, as he liked to capture the qualities of dogs that make them appear most like human beings.

Overall, subjects of his photographs show thoughtful emotion and carefree playfulness. His images are among the most celebrated of the twentieth century. Erwitt's contributions to photography have been recognized in journalism, film, and art.

CHAPTER 3

SCULPTORS

Sculpture may be the oldest form of art. Petroglyphs, or rock carvings, can be found on cave walls around the world. Some date back to 14,800 years ago.[1] The materials ancient peoples used for sculpture included stones, rocks, clay, wood, or metals. Today, sculpture materials include plastics, metals, fabrics, ceramics, glass, and silicone rubber.

For thousands of years, people made sculptures for several reasons but mostly for prayer or worship. Today sculptors use many different themes in their work, including immigration. For instance, the people in Bruno Catalano's sculptures usually hold bags or luggage. Also, large sections of the figures are cut out, allowing the people to blend into the outdoor landscapes. The sculptures remind one of travel, home, and human migration. The 20-foot-tall (6-meter-tall) *Inflatable Refugee* by Belgian visual artist team Schellekens & Peleman is another example of an immigration theme in sculpture. The artists created it to raise awareness about refugees and the crises they experience.

When sculptors bring up immigration in their works, many do so from personal experience. Famous sculptors such as Louise Bourgeois, Eva Hesse, and Stefan Pokorny all have immigrant backgrounds.

Humans have created rock carvings and sculptures for thousands of years. This work of Dravidian architecture in Mamallapuram, India is an example. Known as *Descent of the Ganges*, it was carved out of rock in the seventh and eighth centuries.

LOUISE BOURGEOIS

Louise Bourgeois was a surrealist sculptor and artist known for her large spider sculptures. The themes of the sculptures were often autobiographical and linked to her troubled childhood.

Louise Bourgeois was born in Paris, France, on December 25, 1911. She was named after her father, Louis, who had wanted a son. When she was a few years old, the family moved to the town of Choisy-le-Roi.

Louise was very close to her mother, Josephine, and she helped her with the family tapestry repair business by sketching ruined or missing parts of the tapestries, or wall hangings. Louise sewed, repaired, and cleaned the tapestries.[2] When the flu made her mother very sick, Louise's father started having an affair with their live-in governess and English tutor, Sadie Gordon Richmond. The situation upset Louise, and she grew up to have bad memories of her father's affairs with other women also. But the memories gave her subject matter for her art.[3]

ICONIC IMMIGRANT SCULPTURE: THE STATUE OF LIBERTY

The Statue of Liberty is perhaps the most famous sculpture in the world as well as one that represents America's core values of freedom, democracy, and immigration. It has served as a great symbol of freedom for the many millions of immigrants who came into New York Harbor through Ellis Island as they arrived in America. The idea of the statue first came about in 1865 when a French author and activist named Edouard de Laboulaye suggested a monument for the United States. In 1876, Frederic Auguste Bartholdi was hired to create a sculpture to celebrate the one-hundred-year anniversary of the United States' Declaration of Independence. It has become a popular tourist attraction, with as many as five million people visiting the Statue of Liberty each year.

To help with the efforts to raise money for the statue, Emma Lazarus wrote a famous poem, "The New Colossus," in 1883. Today the poem is on a bronze plaque inside the statue's museum. The most famous and memorable lines about coming to the United States for freedom and opportunity are, "Give me your tired, your poor, Your huddled masses yearning to breathe free, The wretched refuse of your teeming shore. Send these, the homeless, tempest-tost to me, I lift my lamp beside the golden door!"

The Statue of Liberty quickly became an iconic symbol for freedom and liberty around the world. Immigrants often saw the famous statue as they approached New York when first arriving in America.

Before becoming an artist, however, Bourgeois studied philosophy and math at Paris's Lycée Fénelon and then at the Sorbonne.[4] Her mother died in 1932, which inspired her to begin studying art.[5] From 1935 to1938, Bourgeois studied with several teachers at different studios in Paris. At first, she worked as a painter and produced prints, but then her favorite teacher, the painter and sculptor Fernand Léger, suggested she focus on sculpture.[6] Her good English—a result of her English governess—helped her to earn money as a translator in Léger's studio to pay for her art classes.

While she was running a small print shop near her parents' business, she met an American art-history student, Robert Goldwater. They married in 1938 and moved to New York. Bourgeois continued to study painting and sculpture with artist Vaclav Vytlacil. She then moved on to the Art Students League.[7]

Bourgeois started psychoanalysis, or psychological counseling, in 1952 and combined it with her art for much of the next thirty years. She became an American citizen in 1955,[8] and through her husband's many art connections, she met artists such as Max Ernst, Marcel Duchamp, André Breton, and Joan Miró.[9]

Bourgeois's work was very personal and often used mythology, symbols, shapes, and objects she found. Her art touched upon her struggles, her mother, and early feminist ideas of womanhood. Her sculptures of spiders, which she said represented her mother, are some of her most famous works. Her most well-known spider sculpture, *Maman*, is a 30-foot-tall (9-meter-tall) bronze sculpture, completed in 1999. The sculpture is permanently located at the Tate Modern, a modern art gallery in London. Another popular spider sculpture, *Spider*, is made from a variety of materials such as steel, tapestry, wood, glass, fabric, rubber, silver, gold, and bone. The piece is of a large spider with a cage located underneath. Because of her spider sculptures, Bourgeois was nicknamed "Spiderwoman."[10]

Louise Bourgeois poses in front of her bronze wall relief sculpture, *Spider IV, 1996.* This image was used in the poster for the 2008 documentary, *Louise Bourgeois: The Spider, the Mistress and the Tangerine.*

According to Bourgeois, "Like a spider, my mother was a weaver. My family was in the business of tapestry restoration, and my mother was in charge of the workshop. Like spiders, my mother was very clever. Spiders are friendly presences that eat mosquitoes. We know that mosquitoes spread diseases and are therefore unwanted. So, spiders are helpful and protective, just like my mother."[11]

Bourgeois was seventy-one years old when she had her first retrospective, which is an exhibit that covers an artist's whole career, at New York City's Museum of Modern Art in 1982.[12] She died on May 31, 2010, at the age of ninety-eight. Today, she is remembered as one of the most important women sculptors of our time and as an early feminist who focused on women's issues that society previously ignored.

EVA HESSE

Eva Hesse was a sculptor and artist known for her use of materials such as rope, wire, fiberglass, polymers, latex, plastics, and found objects. Found objects simply mean materials artists have discovered on their own, either by accident or on purpose. Hesse's work is part of the Post-Minimalism art movement, which she is often given credit for starting.

Eva Hesse was born on January 11, 1936, in Hamburg, Germany. Her family was Jewish and experienced prejudice and mistreatment in Germany before World War II started. Her father, Wilhelm, was not allowed to work, and her mother, Ruth, suffered from depression. Eva and her sister, Helen, were moved to safety when she was two years old.[13] The entire family then escaped Nazi Germany in 1939 and arrived in New York City.

Eva's mother's depression became worse, and in 1944 her parents separated, followed by their divorce in 1945. The following year, when Eva was only ten, her mother committed suicide after learning her parents died in the Holocaust. The tragic loss of her mother deeply saddened Hesse.

Sculptor Eva Hesse works on one of her sculptures of rubber-dipped strings and rope. This photo was taken in 1969, just one year before Hesse died.

She went on to study at the New York City School of Industrial Art, which is now known as the High School of Art and Design. She then graduated from Pratt Institute in 1952 and studied at Cooper Union from 1954 to 1957. From there, she graduated from Yale University School of Art and Architecture in 1959.[14] Afterward, Hesse became an intern at Seventeen magazine, and the publication ran an article about her artwork.[15]

In 1961, Hesse married the sculptor Tom Doyle, and they moved to Germany. There, Hesse created her first sculptures from rope and found objects, which would become the style for which she was known. After returning to New York in 1965, Hesse and Doyle separated. The following year she began to include fiberglass and latex in her work. This caused her to become very popular, and in the late 1960s, she had many gallery shows and sold much of her work to art collectors.

Many of Hesse's sculptures looked like cells under a microscope. Some of her early sculptures were wall hangings in which ropes, shapes, and materials projected off the wall, often hanging down to the floor. These wall pieces bridged the gap between paintings and sculptures. Hesse's larger works hung from the walls and ceilings of galleries and museums and took up so much space that people could walk around or beneath them.

Her art could not easily be put into a category, including the category of sculpture. She made her 1966 hanging sculpture *Not Yet* from net bags, clear polyethylene sheeting, paper, metal weights, and string. The sculpture looked like a creature caught in fishing nets or perhaps even fishnet stockings. Hesse would use different styles of art in her pieces and juxtapose (place side by side) items that didn't necessarily fit together so that the viewer might find interesting meanings in her work.[16]

THE IMMIGRANTS

Spanish-born sculptor Luis Sanguino made the sculpture *The Immigrants* in 1973.[17] The bronze sculpture, located in Manhattan's Battery Park, shows a group of people from different ethnic backgrounds huddled together. Among them are an eastern European Jew, a freed African slave, a priest, and a worker. The sculpture celebrates the diversity of New York City and the struggle of many immigrants who have come to the United States.

Samuel Rudin first called for the sculpture to be made in the early 1970s as a memorial to his parents, who immigrated to the United States in the late 1800s. Although Rudin died in 1975, his family helped with the sculpture's installation at the park. It was dedicated on May 4, 1983.

Luis Sanguino was born in 1934 in Barcelona, Spain. Hundreds of his sculptures and monuments are located around Mexico, Spain, and the United States. *The Immigrants* is one of his best-known sculptures.

In 1968, Hesse began teaching at the School of Visual Arts. During this time, headaches that had bothered her for several years became worse.[18] After a trip to the hospital, she learned that she had a large brain tumor. She had several operations, while continuing to produce art, but they didn't help. She died on May 29, 1970, at the age of thirty-four.

In 2016, a documentary film about her life, called *Eva Hesse*, came out. Directed by Marcie Begleiter, the film documents Hesse's art, her important but short-lived career, and many details about her life. The film is evidence that the public continues to appreciate Hesse's sculptures.

STEFAN POKORNY

Stefan Pokorny is a sculptor, artist, and businessman known for the hand-sculpted tabletop landscapes made by his company, Dwarven Forge, to play games such as *Dungeons and Dragons Pathfinder*, *Call of Cthulhu*, and *Star Wars*. *Dungeons and Dragons*, also known as *D&D*, is a fantasy storytelling game that Gary Gygax and Dave Arneson created in 1974.

Stefan Pokorny was born in Seoul, South Korea, on December 25, 1966, to a Korean mother and an American father. A European couple adopted him in 1969. His adoptive father, Jan, was from Prague, Czechoslovakia. His adoptive mother, Marise, was from Rome, Italy. After they both immigrated to the United States and married, they became Stefan's legal guardians.[19]

Stefan's father was an architect and often took the family to Europe during the summers. There, Stefan saw a variety of beautiful art and architecture. His parents also loved art and gave him art supplies at a young age to keep him busy. In the 1980s, he went to sleepaway camp and learned about the fantasy game *Dungeons and Dragons*. Stefan fell in love with *D&D* and continued playing throughout his life.

Stefan Pokorny (*left*), with writer-director Josh Bishop (*center*) and writer-producer Nate Taylor (*right*), of the documentary film, *The Dwarvenaut*. Pokorny's company, Dwarven Forge, creates pre-painted miniature terrain for use with tabletop roleplaying games.

While growing up in New York City, Stefan sometimes acted up and was even kicked out of high school. His parents convinced him to enroll in New York City's High School of Art and Design,[20] where he became a student during his sophomore year. Once back in school, Stefan developed a good relationship with one art teacher, Irwin Greenberg, who ran an early morning painting class for students to attend before school started.[21] Stefan attended the class and, through the help of his new mentor, excelled in art. He graduated from high school in 1985 with three first-place medals in painting, airbrush, and poetry.

He then went on to study painting and sculpture at the Hartford Art School in Connecticut, where he earned a degree in painting and won the Julius Hallgarten Prize in 1992.[22]

Pokorny continued to play *Dungeons and Dragons* with friends, but rather than playing the game on flat two-dimensional maps, he built three-dimensional cardboard caves and buildings. Inspired by his day job painting collectibles, Pokorny decided to sculpt three-dimensional landscapes, or terrain, for games.

Pokorny started his company, Dwarven Forge, in 1996 and began selling his pre-painted scenery to fans of *Dungeons and Dragons*. He also set up a booth at Gen Con, the biggest tabletop gaming convention in North America. Once the convention opened, his gaming landscapes sold out in just four hours! Pokorny then went on to use the popular website Kickstarter.com to raise money for his growing company. In 2016, director Josh Bishop released a documentary, *The Dwarvenaut*, about Pokorny and his work at Dwarven Forge.

Pokorny has also opened a gallery in Brooklyn, New York, called Zaltar's Gallery of Fantastical Art. He continues to create art, sculpt, run his company, and play *Dungeons and Dragons*.

CHAPTER 4

MIXED MEDIA ARTISTS

Mixed media is artwork created by using different types of materials. The art form started around 1912,[1] when Pablo Picasso and Georges Braque began to try out collage. Since then, the term "mixed media" has grown to include just about anything. Today, mixed media artists use everything from paint to metal to plastics or wood. They even use found objects. Famous immigrant artists Yayoi Kusama and Yoko Ono have both used mixed media in their work.

YAYOI KUSAMA

Yayoi Kusama is a mixed media artist known for her colorful works featuring polka dots, performance art, painting, music, and sculptures. She lived and worked in the United States for fifteen years. Kusama dressed much like her artwork, often wearing a bright red wig and outfits with huge polka dots.

Yayoi Kusama was born on March 22, 1929, in Matsumoto, Japan. Her father, Kamon, and her mother, Shigeru, owned a plant nursery.[2] Her family was very strict, and she had a difficult childhood.

When Yayoi was ten, she started painting. She liked to use polka dots in her work because she saw them in hallucinations, or visions. Her mother

Yayoi Kusama poses in front of one of her paintings at her *I Who Have Arrived in Heaven* show. The photo was taken during the exhibition press preview at the David Zwirner Art Gallery on November 7, 2013 in New York City.

didn't want her to be an artist and took all of her art supplies away. She wanted Yayoi to live as a traditional Japanese woman, not as an artist. This meant marriage and children.

But Kusama followed her dreams. In 1948, when she was nineteen, she left home and started studying Japanese Nihonga painting at the Kyoto Municipal School of Arts and Crafts. She studied there for one year and then created a large amount of work in a very short time period. In 1952 alone, more than five hundred pieces of her artwork[3] were exhibited.

In 1955, Kusama began writing letters to American artist Georgia O'Keeffe, whose work she loved. She sent the famous artist fourteen watercolor paintings. Afterward, Kusama's work made it into the 18th Biennial International Watercolor Exhibition at the Brooklyn Museum in New York. In 1956, with the help of Dr. Shiho Nishimaru, Kusama received a visa to allow her to travel to the United States. Before she left, she destroyed thousands of pieces of her art. After arriving in the United States in 1958, Kusama joined the Art Students League of New York to get a student visa and remain in the country.[4]

IMMIGRATION ARTIFACTS EXHIBIT

Undocumented immigrants who walk across the border from Mexico into the United States often face a difficult journey. According to the International Organization for Migration, more than six thousand such immigrants have died while crossing the desert.[5]

The Undocumented Migration Project began in 2008 when Jason De León, an assistant professor of anthropology at the University of Michigan, began to collect the items migrants left behind in Arizona's Sonoran Desert. With the help of his students, he has since collected more than ten thousand items. They include backpacks, water bottles, sneakers, clothing, photos, letters, and notebooks.

In 2013, Amanda Krugliak, an artist and the curator of the University of Michigan's Institute for the Humanities, reached out to De León about featuring his collection in an exhibit. Along with photographer Richard Barnes, they created a multimedia exhibition, *State of Exception*. It has traveled around the country, giving attention to the problems of undocumented immigrants.

According to a video interview with Kusama, she went to the top of the Empire State Building when she arrived in New York. As she looked around the city from the skyscraper, she promised herself that she would one day become a famous artist.

Kusama then made her famous *Infinity Net* paintings, which are made up of thousands of tiny shapes. Both Minimalism and Pop Art themes appear in her work from this period.

By the early 1960s, Kusama's work was shown in different galleries and museums around New York City. She became good friends with artist Eva Hesse after moving her studio into Hesse's building.

Through an art dealer, Kusama met artist Joseph Cornell and started dating[6] him. During this time, she displayed her work with artists Claes Oldenburg and Andy Warhol and became a US citizen in 1966.[7]

Kusama then began creating large mirrored works of art to explore the theme of infinity, or time without end. Some of her pieces took up entire rooms. She also staged performance art (which includes acting, dancing, and singing) that opposed war.

In 1973, she returned to Japan. Four years later, she moved into a mental hospital, where she has lived for more than forty years.[8] She entered the hospital because she has endured nervous disorders and hallucinations since childhood. During her time there, Kusama has continued to create artwork in her studio in nearby Shinjuku, Tokyo.

In 1989, Kusama exhibited her pieces in New York and England. Since then she has had numerous art shows. In 2006, Kusama received the Japanese Art Association's Praemium Imperiale prize for painting. She also displayed her work at the Whitney Museum of American Art in 2012.

Yayoi Kusama's exciting artwork has proven to be ahead of its time. Today, she continues to make art. As new generations of artists discover her work, she has only become more popular.

YOKO ONO

Yoko Ono is a mixed media artist known for her performance art, music, films, poetry, sculpture, and paintings. She became a celebrity after her marriage to John Lennon of the 1960s rock band the Beatles. She was also a member of the art group Fluxus, made up of artists, musicians, and poets who staged performances.

Before meeting and marrying rock music legend John Lennon of the Beatles, Yoko Ono was already a multimedia artist. She performed in galleries around New York City in the late 1960s.

Yoko Ono was born on February 18, 1933, in Tokyo, Japan. She grew up the eldest of three children and came from a creative and wealthy family. Her father, Yeisuke Ono, was a banker who had also trained as a classical pianist. Her mother, Isoko, was a painter and musician who played nine instruments.[9] Her parents wanted her to become a classically trained pianist like her father, so Yoko started piano lessons at age four and took opera lessons as well.

She did not meet her father until she was two years old because he'd been away on business. Her family moved to San Francisco but returned to Japan after three years. They went on to live in the United States temporarily during the years leading up to World War II, but Yoko remained in Japan. She was in Tokyo when the US bombed the city in 1945.

Six years later, Ono became the first woman to study philosophy at Tokyo's Gakushuin University. But she did not finish her studies and left Japan to be with her family in Scarsdale, New York. There, she attended Sarah Lawrence College and began dating Toshi Ichiyanagi, a student at the famous Juilliard music school.[10] During this time, she wrote her first piece of music, *Secret Piece*.

Once again, Ono did not finish her studies. She ended up marrying Ichiyanagi and working as an artist in Manhattan. She and her husband moved into a downtown loft, an open room beneath the roof of a building. At her loft, Ono wrote poetry and held performances with music composer La Monte Young. Her performances often required viewers to participate. A piece she created in 1960, *Painting to Be Stepped On*, required viewers to walk across a painting placed on the floor.

During this period, Ono became involved with the group of artists known as Fluxus who wanted to change the world through art.[11] With this group, often in her loft, Ono continued to write poetry and create performances called "happenings." George Maciunas, the founder of Fluxus, gave Ono her first solo show at his gallery in 1961. Around this time, Ono separated from her husband.

In 1962, Ono moved to Japan. There, she met filmmaker Anthony Cox and married him in 1963. The next year the couple returned to the United States, where her performance pieces grew more popular. *Cut Piece* stands out as one of her most famous early performances. As Ono sat, participants were asked to use scissors to cut pieces of her dress off. The performance was a statement about violence and is now considered to be an important work of feminist art.

In 1966, Ono and Cox moved to London and started working on a film together. There, she met John Lennon of the Beatles during her art show at the Indica Gallery. During the show, Lennon had to climb up a ladder to read small text on the ceiling that stated, "Yes!" Afterward, Ono and Lennon worked together on art and film projects. After divorcing their spouses, they got married on March 20, 1969.

During their honeymoon, Ono and Lennon held their famous "bed-in" at their hotel room in Amsterdam to promote peace. They

MEMES: MULTIMEDIA ART WITH NO BORDERS

Memes. You might know the term, but what exactly is a meme? British scientist Richard Dawkins introduced the word in 1976, when he used it to describe ideas or behaviors that spread from person to person or from culture to culture.

Today, the word "meme" also refers to small digital files, usually jpeg pictures, animated GIFs, or videos that spread online through social media. Memes are a modern form of multimedia art, and their subject matter can be artistic, political, comedic, and more. Like much art that we see, memes get people to think about the world in which they live.

then collaborated on an album together, *Yoko Ono/Plastic Ono Band,* in 1970. On March 24, 1973, Ono became a permanent resident of the United States. John Lennon became a permanent resident in 1975.[12] Their child, Sean, was born October 9, 1975. Lennon then stopped making music so he could stay home to raise Sean. But he and Ono released another album together, *Double Fantasy,* in 1980.

On December 8, 1980, a crazed fan, Mark David Chapman, shot and killed Lennon in Manhattan. Ono stood just a few feet away from Lennon when the tragedy happened outside their apartment building. Chapman was sentenced to twenty years to life in prison. Upon hearing news of Lennon's shocking death, ten thousand fans filled the streets outside his home in Central Park and held a ten-minute silent vigil on the morning of December 14. In the years after

Yoko Ono and her husband John Lennon pose for a picture after preparing her first one-woman show, *This is Not Here...An Exhibit of Conceptual Works of Art.*

Lennon's death, Ono released some of his previously unreleased music. She also helped create a memorial in his honor, Strawberry Fields, in New York City's Central Park.

Ono continued on as a recording and performance artist in the 1980s. Her 1981 album, *Season of Glass*, was a very personal reaction to Lennon's death. The cover of the album was a photograph of Lennon's bloodied eyeglasses beside a half-filled glass of water. In the years that followed, Ono has gone on to have several shows at the Whitney Museum of American Art and the Japan Society Gallery, both in New York City.

Yoko Ono remains an important artist whose work inspires and influences her peers and fans around the world.

CHAPTER 5

COMIC BOOK ARTISTS

omic books aren't just for kids anymore; adults enjoy them, too! These hand-drawn tales featuring powerful superheroes and villains are big business today. North American sales of comic books and graphic novels topped more than $1 billion in 2015,[1] according to some estimates. Also, comic book conventions around the United States have had huge attendance in recent years, and many colleges now offer degrees in comic book art and illustration. College students may even read graphic novels in their literature classes.

Comic book artists, which include a number of immigrants, are the driving force behind such trends. So, how have immigrants left their mark on comics? The life and works of Joe Shuster, Sergio Aragonés, and Art Spiegelman reveal how immigrant comic-book artists have made a difference.

JOE SHUSTER

Joe Shuster was a comic book artist who teamed up with writer Jerry Siegel to create perhaps the most famous superhero ever—Superman. Shuster's illustrations of Superman led to the growth of the multibillion-dollar comic book industry.

The creators of Superman, Jerry Siegel and Joe Shuster, helped to launch the superhero comic industry. They also became famous for selling the rights to Superman for a mere $65 each in 1938.

Joe Shuster was born on July 10, 1914, in Toronto, Canada. When he was just nine years old, he helped his family earn money by selling newspapers in Toronto. That same year, Joe's father, Julius, moved the family to Cleveland, Ohio. As a child, Joe enjoyed drawing and liked to read the Sunday comic strips in the newspaper. When he ran out of drawing paper and couldn't afford to buy more, he used scraps of tissue paper from his father's business[2] to sketch his drawings.

As a student at Glenville High School in 1930, he met writer Jerry Siegel. They both worked on the school newspaper.[3] With Siegel writing and Shuster drawing, they created two early comics for the paper, *Goober the Mighty*, which was similar to Tarzan, and *Interplanetary Police*, which was similar to Buck Rogers.[4] The pair continued working together and created an early version of Superman in which the main character was a villain, not a hero.

The two would go on to create a professional comic about Superman. Shuster developed the artwork for the project, while Siegel wrote the stories.[5] According to a 2013 article from the *New Yorker*, Shuster said, "Our concept would be to combine the best traits of all the heroes of history."[6]

Superman was first published in the comic book *Action Comics* in June 1938. The character went on to become very popular. In 1940, a Superman radio series began, and by the next year, the character was the star of his own animated cartoon.[7] By the 1950s, a live-action TV show about the superhero debuted.

Despite the great success of the character they invented, Siegel and Shuster didn't make a profit from their creation. They had sold their original thirteen-page story for $130 and were hired to continue working on the comic for $10 per page. They even sold the rights to the story and the character to DC Comics. When Siegel and Shuster sued DC for more money in 1947, the company fired them. Shuster eventually left the comic book business.

In the years that followed, Superman would become more popular, leading to an industry full of other superheroes with unique powers, such as Wonder Woman, the X-Men, and Spider-Man. By the 1970s, Shuster lived in Queens, New York, jobless and legally blind. In 1975, DC Comics finally agreed to pay Shuster and Siegel each $20,000 in yearly pensions. The comic book giant eventually raised the sum to $30,000 and gave the duo credit for

UNDOCUMENTED IMMIGRANT SUPERHEROES

Undocumented immigration in the United States has long sparked controversy. To be undocumented means that an immigrant has entered the United States without the paperwork that legally gives him or her permission to be in the country. It may take years to get such permission, and some immigrants are in desperate situations that lead them to set out for the United States whether or not they have permission. While many Americans support these immigrants, large numbers of US citizens do not.

San Francisco artist Neil Rivas is using his work to draw attention to the issue. His 2012 art series, *Illegal Superheroes*, shows popular comic book characters on fake "wanted" posters because they are "aliens," making them undocumented immigrants. Superman, Wonder Woman, Wolverine, and the Transformers Autobot leader Optimus Prime are just a few of the fifteen "Most Wanted" characters. The posters ask viewers to contact the "San Francisco ICE Field Office" if they spot any of these famous characters. There is also a fake website that goes along with the posters—icedish.org.

creating Superman. Joe Shuster died in 1992, and Jerry Siegel died in 1996. The cancelled check for $130 that DC Comics first paid Siegel and Shuster sold at a 2012 auction for $160,000. Today, Superman remains a multimillion-dollar franchise.

SERGIO ARAGONÉS

Sergio Aragonés is a cartoonist known for his *Mad Magazine* comic strips and his comic book character Groo the Wanderer.

Sergio Aragonés was born in 1937 in Castellon, Spain. During the Spanish Civil War, his family moved to Mexico. By the third grade, he started drawing cartoons, which sometimes upset his schoolteachers.[8] Later, Sergio fell in love with pantomime (a theatrical style in which silent entertainers make movements) after seeing French actor and mime Marcel Marceau perform. The silent performances had a big impact on Sergio and would later inspire his wordless comic strips.

As a young man, Aragonés met famous film director Alejandro Jodorowsky and worked under him. He then went on to study architecture at the University of Mexico. His love of comics continued, and in 1962 he moved to the United States. He had only $20 and a portfolio filled with his artwork when he first arrived in New York City. What little work he landed did not come easy, and Aragonés had to take odd jobs at restaurants and a coffee shop.[9] He tried to sell his work but had difficulty doing so. In an article in the *Los Angeles Times*, Aragonés was quoted as saying, "They would look at my work and they would say, 'These cartoons are crazy, you should go to *Mad!*'"

Mad is a comic magazine that began in 1952.[10] Aragonés wasn't sure *Mad* would accept his work because the publication was so well known and respected, but he found the courage to go there with his artwork. At the magazine, he quickly found success. His new coworkers welcomed him, helped him learn English, and made him feel part of the "family."[11] Aragonés's first comic series ran in the seventy-sixth issue of *Mad* in 1963, "A Mad Look at the U.S. Space Effort."[12] His hilariously drawn series "A Mad Look at…" continued for decades. The strip pokes fun of everything from movies and TV shows to politics and social issues.

Mad Magazine comic artist Sergio Aragonés autographs one of his comics at a convention held at the Stockton Arena in Stockton, California on August 20, 2016. Aragonés continues to produce cartoons for the satirical magazine.

In the 1980s, Aragonés joined writer Mark Evanier to create the comic book *Groo the Wanderer*, which spoofs fantasy barbarians, especially Conan the Barbarian. The comic series went on to become one of the longest running team efforts in comic book history.

As Aragonés's work won him many fans, he began to win awards as well. His honors include the National Cartoonist's Society's Reuben Award, the Will Eisner Hall of Fame Award, and an award named after him, the Comic Art Professional Society's Sergio Award. Today, Aragonés continues to work on his comic book creations. He lives and works in Ojai, California.

WAS WINSOR MCCAY AN IMMIGRANT?

Winsor McCay is often regarded as the father of comic strips and animation. He is best known for his comic strip *Little Nemo in Slumberland* and for his 1914 animated short film called *Gertie the Dinosaur*.

There is still some disagreement today about exactly where and when Winsor McCay was born. When McCay was older he claimed to be born at Spring Lake, Michigan, on September 26, 1871. McCay did grow up in Michigan and started drawing there as a child. But biographer John Canemaker discovered that McCay once told a census taker that he was born in 1869.[13] McCay's tombstone also has a birthdate of 1869 inscribed on it. Michigan census records from 1870 and 1880 show that he was born in Canada in 1867. Canemaker believed McCay's mother might have given birth to him while visiting her family near the city of Woodstock in Ontario, Canada, in 1867. Given these different reports, it is unclear whether McCay should be considered an immigrant artist.[14]

ART SPIEGELMAN

Art Spiegelman is an author and comic book artist best known for his underground comic anthology *Raw* and his groundbreaking Holocaust-based graphic novel *Maus*, which won a Pulitzer Prize in 1992.

Art Spiegelman was born on February 14, 1948, in Stockholm, Sweden. Both of his parents were survivors of the Holocaust, the

68

Comic artist and author Art Spiegelman is best known for his Pulitzer Prize-winning graphic novel, *Maus: A Survivor's Tale*. The work was based on his father's firsthand account of surviving the Holocaust during World War II.

killing of six million Jews by Germany's Nazis during World War II. Spiegelman's father, Vladek, was born in the village of Dabrowa, in Silesia, Poland, in 1906. His mother, Anja Zylberberg, was born in Sosnowiec, Poland, in 1912. The two first met in 1935 and were married on February 14, 1937. Shortly afterwards, their first son, Richieu, was born. Because of World War II, many family members were separated from each other, including Spiegelman's parents and Richieu. In 1943, to prevent Richieu from the horrors of the Nazi concentration camps, a family member poisoned him and other children to death.

Before becoming known for his graphic novel *Maus*, Art Spiegelman worked as an illustrator. He created many of the images used in the 1980s popular trading cards, *Garbage Pail Kids*.

In 1944 and 1945, Spiegelman's parents were taken to separate concentration camps. After the war, miraculously, Anja and Vladek reunited in Sosnowiec, Poland. They then had their second son, Art, in Stockholm, Sweden, in 1948. Later that same year, the three immigrated to the United States and became citizens. After first moving to Pennsylvania, they relocated to Queens, New York, in 1955.

Art grew up in Rego Park, Queens, and became interested in drawing comic books. He found inspiration in comics he enjoyed, such as in *Mad Magazine*. In 1961, he started studying art at New York City's High School of Art and Design. He then studied art and philosophy at Harpur College, but his mental health began to suffer, forcing him to drop out of school in 1968. Spiegelman became a patient at Binghamton State Mental Hospital for a month, during which time his mother committed suicide.

Spiegelman then began working professionally as an artist for the Topps Chewing Gum Company. There for two decades, he helped to create the popular trading cards, *Wacky Packages* and *Garbage Pail Kids*.[15] In 1975, he moved back to New York and continued his work on underground comics. He met Francoise Mouly, marrying her on July 12, 1977.

It took Spiegelman thirteen years to finish his most noteworthy accomplishment, *Maus*. He created thousands of sketches and drawings for the graphic novel. In *Maus*, Jewish people are drawn as mice and the Germans as cats. Spiegelman used this metaphor because during the Holocaust, the Germans often referred to the Jews as vermin, or animals. The story even includes Spiegelman interviewing his father about the Holocaust.

When Spiegelman first tried to publish *Maus*, many publishers rejected the graphic novel, mostly because they did not understand the serious subject matter in comic form or were unsure how to market it. Spiegelman saved many of his rejection letters.

Eventually, Pantheon published *Maus: A Survivor's Tale* in 1986, and it won several awards. In 1991, *Maus: A Survivor's Tale II: And Here My Troubles Began* appeared in installments in the publication the *Jewish Forward*. Pantheon published the sequel also. The two-volume set of *Maus* won the Pulitzer Prize in 1992 and led the public to view graphic novels as serious works of literature.

Today, Spiegelman lives in New York City with his wife and children. He continues to work as a writer and an illustrator for publications such as the *New York Times, the Village Voice*, and the *New Yorker*.[16]

CHAPTER 6

FILM AND ANIMATION ARTISTS

Some of the most unsung artists of our time work tirelessly behind the scenes at their craft and create the art and animation that entertains the masses. In film, artists use their imaginations to make the director's vision reality. Their works are used to create landscapes, fantasy worlds, spaceships, costumes, aliens, and new characters. Animation artists invent entire films from scratch by imagining backgrounds, characters, vehicles, and clothing. Artists Doug Chiang and Genndy Tartakovsky are two of the many artists who've made a huge impact on Hollywood, and they both happen to be immigrants.

DOUG CHIANG

Doug Chiang is a film production designer and concept artist known for his contributions to movies such as *Rogue One: A Star Wars Story* (2016) and *War of the Worlds* (2005). Much of his art is used for special effects in movies.[1]

Chiang was born on February 16, 1962, in Taipei, Taiwan. His family immigrated to Dearborn, Michigan, in 1968. They then moved to Westland, Michigan, just outside Detroit, in 1972. As a

Star Wars concept artist Doug Chiang attends the world premiere of the film *Rogue One*. The film debuted at the Pantages Theatre on December 10, 2016 in Hollywood, California.

child, Doug became interested in films and by 1974, when he was in middle school, he made his first short animated film. Soon he set up a basement studio in his house, and over the next two years completed over a dozen shorts.

In 1976, when Doug was in high school, he produced a short film called *Gladiator*. After seeing the films *Star Wars* and *The Golden Voyage of Sinbad*, he decided he wanted to become a stop-motion animator. This is an animation technique that makes an inanimate object look like it is moving. He spent much of his time drawing images based on movie scenes. He admired artists Ralph McQuarrie and Joe Johnston, who worked on the original *Star Wars* films. In 1978, Doug made another short film inspired by *Star Wars*. It won him first place in the Michigan Student Film Festival.

In 1979, while attending John Glenn High School, Chiang had stomach surgery and was hospitalized for many months. He needed eight more surgeries over the course of a year but still graduated from high school in 1981 with honors. Afterward, Chiang studied industrial design at the College for Creative Studies in Detroit.[2] He then went on to study film production at the University of California, Los Angeles (UCLA).

UNRECOGNIZED *BAMBI* ARTIST TYRUS WONG

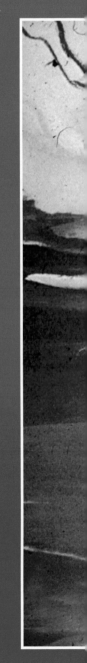

When the Disney classic *Bambi* premiered in 1942, Chinese immigrant Tyrus Wong basically served as the lead illustrator on the film. Despite Wong's major contribution to *Bambi*, he did not get credit. Instead, Disney listed him as just a background artist. One day that would change.

Tyrus Wong was born in China in 1910 and enjoyed painting and drawing at an early age. Tyrus and his father immigrated to the United States when he was only nine years old. His mother and sister remained in China, and he never saw either of them again.[3]

He started working at Disney in 1938 as an "inbetweener," an artist who fills in the animation between key frames. Once production started on *Bambi*, Wong read the book and began creating artwork. Walt Disney liked Wong's moody paintings so much that he had the film's entire style based on his watercolor art.

Because of racism directed at Chinese immigrants in the 1930s and 1940s, Wong never received any real credit for his animation work until he was ninety years old. He was finally named a Disney legend in 2001. The Chinese American Museum in Los Angeles and the Walt Disney Family Museum in San Francisco have both hosted exhibits of Wong's artwork. In 2014, *Tyrus*, a documentary film about Wong, debuted. The artist died the following year at age 106.

Artist Tyrus Wong's art heavily contributed to the overall look and feel of the now classic 1942 animated Disney feature film, *Bambi*.

After completing college, Chiang worked as an illustrator, art director, and storyboard artist. He continued to create art, personal films, and animation. In 1985, his short film *Mental Block* won first prize—a new car—in the FOCUS film competition. In 1985, Chiang started working as a concept designer for the Universal Pictures film *Back to the Future 2*. Later that year, he moved to Northern California and began working as a visual effects art director for the Lucasfilm special effects company, Industrial Light and Magic (ILM). By 1993, Chiang was the creative director for ILM.

In 1995, Chiang worked with a small team put together by George Lucas for the prequels to the original *Star Wars* trilogy. Many of Chiang's concept art pieces and designs were included in the *Star Wars* prequels. A concept is simply an idea. According to an interview with Chiang on thestar.com, "We were designing as he [George Lucas] was writing, which is actually very unusual. I think it's a model that is now used in many films but it was very unusual in the sense that I got to start designing right when he was writing. My job didn't end until the film was up on the screen."[4]

Chiang also worked with director Gareth Edwards on the first stand-alone *Star Wars* film, *Rogue One*. According to a quote from Chiang in the *Toronto Sun*, "I grew up drawing things like X-wings and TIE fighters, and I'm finally getting an opportunity to do that."[5]

Today Chiang is vice president and executive creative director at Lucasfilm, which Disney now owns.[6] He lives in Northern California with his wife and three children.[7]

GENNDY TARTAKOVSKY

Genndy Tartakovsky is an animator, director, writer, and producer known for his animated TV series *Dexter's Laboratory*, *The Powerpuff Girls*, *Samurai Jack*, *Star Wars: The Clone Wars*, and *Sym-Bionic Titan*.

Tartakovsky was born January 17, 1970, in Moscow, Russia. His father, Boris, was a dentist, and his mother, Miriam, was an

ANIME AND MANGA

Anime is a kind of animation produced in Japan. Today, anime and Japanese comics called manga can be found all over the United States, but this wasn't always the case. Anime dates back to the early 1900s, but Japanese animation remained unknown to most people in the United States until the early 1960s. The first Japanese cartoon to come to the United States was *Astro Boy*, which aired on the NBC television network in 1963.[8]

In the 1970s and 1980s, more serious animated series appeared on US television. *Battle of the Planets*, *Star Blazers*, and *Robotech* all became popular with American teens.[9]

Katsuhiro Ôtomo and Hayao Miyazaki directed animated films in the 1980s that are still popular today. For example, Ôtomo's *Akira* and Miyazaki's *Nausicaä of the Valley of the Wind* and *My Neighbor Totoro* continue to entertain Americans.

In 2009, the Japan External Trade Organization found that the value of the American anime market was close to $300 billion.[10] Today, Japanese animation is more popular than ever in the United States, and new Japanese manga comics and anime films come out regularly, continuing to have a huge influence on American comic and animation artists.

assistant principal. Because of prejudice against Jews in Russia then, his family was not treated well. In 1977, when Genndy was seven, his family left Russia.[11] They spent several months in Florence and Rome, Italy, before finally settling in the United States. Genndy began drawing during his few months in Italy. He and his older brother,

Alex, befriended a Russian girl who liked to sketch street scenes of people and merchants. After meeting the girl, the brothers tried to copy her drawings.[12]

In the United States, Genndy and his family first lived in Ohio, where he learned about comic books. Tartakovsky remembers buying his first comic book, *The Super Friends*, from a rack of comics at a 7-Eleven convenience store. He soon fell in love with comic books, copying different cartoons and superheroes. He also spent much of his free time watching cartoons on TV and learning about American culture as he watched. Even on mornings before school, Genndy watched TV, which helped him to learn English.[13]

When he was ten years old, his family moved to Chicago, Illinois. He wanted to fit in his new city but had some trouble. Other children teased him because he did not know much about American culture, but he did make some friends with whom he drew comic book characters and superheroes. While a student at Lane Technical College Prep High School, his father died of a heart attack. Afterward, his family did not have much money to support themselves, so Genndy worked many jobs to earn cash.

In 1988, he studied advertising at Columbia College, a large art and film school. After taking an animation class, he switched his major to film. Eventually, Tartakovsky and his close friend Rob Renzetti made plans to attend the California Institute of the Arts (CalArts). The school accepted Tartakovsky, allowing him to take art classes that Columbia didn't offer. At CalArts, Tartakovsky worked on an animated short film that would later become the animated television show *Dexter's Laboratory*.

After graduating in 1992, Tartakovsky moved to Spain and worked on animating *Batman: The Animated Series*. During this time, his mother died, and the company he worked for went bankrupt. Tartakovsky went on to work for Cartoon Network, where officials turned his idea for *Dexter's Laboratory* into a TV show. The first

Genndy Tartakovsky wrote and directed many episodes of the Cartoon Network animated television series *The Powerpuff Girls*. The show featured three superhero sisters, Buttercup, Blossom, and Bubbles, who fought crime in the fictional City of Townsville.

episode was completed in 1995, and the show became a success, with many fans. Tartakovsky later worked on *The Powerpuff Girls* and *Samurai Jack*, both of which became hits.

In 2003, George Lucas hired Tartakovsky to direct an animated series for Cartoon Network, *Star Wars: Clone Wars*. The series was told in small, three-minute segments. Working on *Star Wars* was a childhood dream come true for Tartakovsky.

Tartakovsky then took a seven-year break from TV but returned to create the robot adventure series *Sym-Bionic Titan*. The show's style and storylines are inspired by the TV shows Tartakovsky grew up watching, such as *Battle of the Planets and Robotech*. Meanwhile, Tartakovsky's show *Samurai Jack* returned for its fifth season in March 2017 on Adult Swim, the late night block of animated shows on the Cartoon Network. Tartakovsky remains one of the most important animators alive today.

CHAPTER 7

STREET ARTISTS

Street art, or graffiti, dates back to the earliest art on cave walls. Modern street art started in New York City and Philadelphia during the 1970s. Artists wrote or spray-painted their nicknames, known as "tags," on public walls, highway overpasses, and train cars.[1] Eventually, street art became more creative and artistic, and some of these artists actually sold work in galleries.

By the mid-1980s, New York City street artists such as Keith Haring and Jean-Michel Basquiat (known on the street as SAMO) became very famous. They sold their work to galleries, which led the highbrow art world to take street art more seriously. Over time, street art has continued to become more artistic and political, with artists using their work to weigh in on social issues.

The internet has allowed street art to live forever online. Because cities and business owners often paint over street art on buildings in an effort to reduce graffiti, photographs posted on the internet help fans remember the art before it disappears. Digital images of street art have earned a following around the world.

In the early 1990s, Shepard Fairey and Banksy drew more public attention to street art. Fairey has created images for the cover of *Time* magazine, and

During the 1980s, New York City street artists such as Jean-Michel Basquiat stopped making art in public spaces. Basquiat began showing his art in galleries, which helped to legitimize street art.

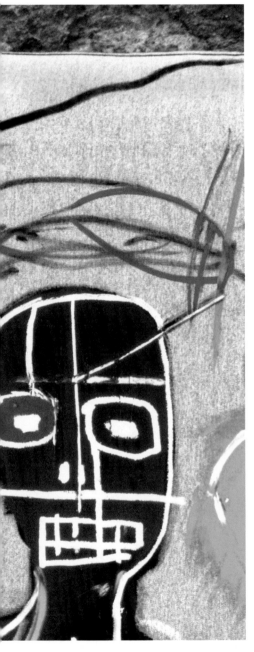

in 2007, auction house Sotheby's in London sold several Banksy pieces for hundreds of thousands of dollars.[2] These events signal that street art has gone mainstream.

While illegal street art remains controversial, business owners and public officials have allowed street artists to cover storefronts, building walls, and public spaces. In addition to street artists like Shepard Fairey and Banksy, Sandra Fabara and Thierry Guetta, both immigrants, have created street art with a large public following.

SANDRA FABARA (LADY PINK)

Lady Pink is a graffiti street artist known for her colorful images, her involvement in the 1980s graffiti book *Subway Art*, and her role in the 1983 film *Wild Style*. Lady Pink stands out as one of the first female graffiti artists.

Born Sandra Fabara in 1964 in Ambato, Ecuador, she came to the United States at age seven with her mother and sister. She grew up in Astoria, Queens, and attended the High School of

Graffiti street artist Lady Pink was photographed at "Marc Ecko's Block Party" on August 24, 2005 in New York City. Lady Pink was one of the first well-known female street artists.

Art and Design in New York City. She started painting graffiti in 1979 at age fifteen when her boyfriend moved back to Puerto Rico. To remember him, she painted his name on train cars. In time, she became known by the street name, or tag, Lady Pink. English romance novels about the rich and powerful inspired her to choose the nickname.[3]

Lady Pink's graffiti style was bright and colorful. It stood out from the work of male graffiti artists, which helped her get noticed. On many evenings, Lady Pink would carefully lower cans of spray paint out of her bedroom window, jump down, and sneak away.[4] She would then meet up with friends and go down into the NYC subway tunnels to paint graffiti art on train cars. One of few female graffiti artists, Lady Pink often competed with boys in the street-art scene.[5]

In the book *Graffiti Word*, Lady Pink was quoted as saying, "At the age of fifteen I started writing graffiti. At first it was to mourn the loss of my first love, so I wrote his name everywhere… I encountered a lot of sexism trying to paint with the boys…I had a very difficult time convincing the guys to even take me to the train yards."

Over the next several years, Lady Pink continued to paint train cars but eventually started painting on canvas,[6] which traditional painters do. In 1983, she starred in Charlie Ahearn's hip-hop film *Wild Style*, which features many musicians and street artists. Many people consider it to be the first hip-hop music film, and it certainly helped make rap popular.

By the time Lady Pink entered high school, she was already displaying her work in art galleries. At twenty-one, she had a solo show, Femmes-Fatales, at Moore College of Art and Design in Philadelphia. Famous institutions such as the Whitney Museum of American Art, the Metropolitan Museum of Art, the Brooklyn Museum, and the Groninger Museum in the Netherlands have also displayed her work. Many of her pieces sell for hundreds of thousands of dollars.[7]

Today Lady Pink no longer does street art unless she is asked. Now she gets help from art students to paint community murals. She also attends different art schools to give presentations, workshops, and teach mural painting to students. Lady Pink and her street artist husband, known as SMITH,[8] ran a mural painting business until he started working as a subway train conductor. But she continues to work in her art studio.

Lady Pink's current works focus on women's rights, gay rights, and other social issues. Her recent works include multiple designs and images that clash with each other. With her husband, she has worked on high-end murals for clients and on murals in low-income neighborhoods. Lady Pink remains one of the leading street artists in the world. She lives and works in New York City.[9]

BANKSY: MYSTERIOUS INTERNATIONAL STREET ARTIST

Who exactly is Banksy? Banksy is a pseudonym, or stage name, for this mysterious international street artist. His works are often political and have appeared in cities and galleries around the world. But the public still doesn't know the real identity of this artist or even if Banksy is male or female. According to several news sources, Banksy might have been born in Bristol, England, around 1974.[10] Mostly created with stencils, the street art linked to Banksy often appeared in Bristol when the artist became popular

Mysterious street artist Banksy opened the satirical Dismaland Bemusement Park on August 28, 2015 in Weston-Super-Mare, England. The burnt-out souvenir ice cream van pictured in front of a decaying castle illustrates Banksy's dark humor.

in the late 1990s. Banksy's street art has criticized war, wealth, inequality, graffiti removal, and more. His work has also made fun of the old-school art world.

Because Banksy's work has appeared all over the world, some people believe a team of international artists[11] may have created the pieces. Bristol, Gaza, Jerusalem, London, Timbuktu, Mali, Los Angeles, Boston, Ontario, Melbourne, New York, New Orleans, San Francisco, Italy, and Alabama are just some of the locations where you can find Banksy street art.

Bansky has also published several books. In 2010, a Banksy documentary about street art called *Exit Through the Gift Shop* premiered. On August 21, 2015, Banksy organized an art project called Dismaland, which pokes fun at Disneyland, in Southwest England. The park featured three galleries with artwork from fifty artists from seventeen countries. Dismaland closed September 27, 2015.[12]

Banksy's identity remains unknown but the artist's work continues to cause controversy, earn praise, and bring attention to important social issues across the world.

THIERRY GUETTA (MR. BRAINWASH)

Mr. Brainwash is a street artist known for his pop art, videography, and large-scale art pieces. He also appeared in the 2010 street-art documentary *Exit Through the Gift Shop*.

Mr. Brainwash was born Thierry Guetta on November 11, 1966, in Garges-lès-Gonesse, Paris, France.[13] His mother died when he was fifteen and shortly afterward, he moved to the United States with his father and several siblings. They settled in Los Angeles,

Street artist Mr. Brainwash paints a wall with a spray paint can during the "Rick Ross and Mr. Brainwash Rather You Than Me Album Listening Experience." The event took place in New York City on March 8, 2017.

California, but his father moved back to France, leaving Thierry and his siblings on their own. Then, their father died. An orphan, Thierry lived in a foreign country where he did not speak the language. He took English as a second language (ESL) classes at Fairfax High School in Los Angeles but eventually dropped out. His ESL teacher, Judith Krischer, remembered him as the class clown.[14]

After quitting school, Guetta took odd jobs, organized parties and events, and worked at a vintage clothing shop in the Venice section of Los Angeles. Soon Guetta opened his own vintage clothing store, buying used clothes from France and reselling them. His business proved to be a success.

Guetta purchased his first video camera in the late 1990s and filmed everything he could. He did not become involved with street art and graffiti until he visited France in 1999, where he discovered that his cousin was the street artist named Space Invader.

Space Invader created images of characters from the 1970s video game *Space Invaders* and put them all over Paris. Guetta began filming street artists as they did their work, usually in the middle of the night.

Guetta then met other street artists, including Shepard Fairey and Banksy, whom he started filming regularly. He also filmed Banksy's 2007 show, *Barely Legal*, in Los Angeles. But his footage turned out to be unusable, and Guetta began creating street art himself. He took on the name Mr. Brainwash, or MBW. In June 2007, he received a $320,000 bank loan to support his art career and upcoming show, *Life Is Beautiful*. Both Shepard Fairey and Banksy promoted the show on their websites. *Life Is Beautiful* opened on June 18, 2008. Guetta lacked formal training as an artist but sold pieces at the event and earned good reviews from critics.

Banksy took Guetta's video footage and created his 2010 street art documentary, *Exit Through the Gift Shop*. Banksy spends part of the documentary focusing on Mr. Brainwash's career as a street artist. The film earned an Oscar nomination for best documentary.

Several critics believe that the artist Mr. Brainwash is not real but a prank Banksy has played on the art community.[15] Shepard Fairey has denied Mr. Brainwash is a prank and includes information about the artist on his website. Mr. Brainwash has appeared in several articles, reviews, and in art shows in different cites.

BORDER WALL ART

The border between the United States and Mexico has been a source of much controversy. During his presidential campaign, Donald Trump promised to build a wall along the almost 2,000-mile (3,218-km) border between the two countries. Until 1969, there was no wall or barrier between the United States and Mexico. Today, a fence runs along about 650 miles (1,046 km) of the border. Many artists have used their work to protest the barrier and Trump's promise to build a wall along the entire border.

Guillermo Galindo has collected objects found along the border, and Richard Misrach, a musician from Mexico City, has

The US border with Mexico is almost 2,000 miles long. It spans from the Gulf of Mexico to the Pacific Ocean. Artistic murals, such as this one in Tijuana, Mexico are common along the 700-mile fenced portion of the border.

turned them into musical instruments. They call their project *Border Cantos*.

In 2009, artist M. Jenea Sanchez made a quilt on the border itself. She used various fabrics, including some she found. She called her project *Border Tapestry*.

In 2011, artist Ana Teresa Fernández from San Francisco painted a 30-foot (9-m) section of the border fence to match the color of the sky so that the fence would seem to disappear in that section.[16] The project, *Borrando la Frontera*, has become well known. And in April 2016, several groups painted parts of the border wall blue in Mexicali, Agua Prieta, and Ciudad Juárez.

German photographer Stefan Falke created the photo project *LA FRONTERA: Artists along the US Mexican Border* in 2008. Falke traveled to many locations and photographed artists living and working along the border. Photos from his project have made the news and been exhibited worldwide.[17]

In 2011, photographer Glen Friedman sued Mr. Brainwash for using a picture he took of rap group Run-D.M.C. without permission.[18] Mr. Brainwash lost the case and, in the process, left little doubt that he is a real person and artist. Despite his setback in court, Mr. Brainwash's art continues to win praise in both the underground street-art scene and the traditional art industry.

CHAPTER NOTES

INTRODUCTION

1. United States Census Bureau, "1850 Fast Facts," https://www.census.gov/history/www/through_the_decades/fast_facts/1850_fast_facts.html.
2. Anna Brown and Renee Stepler, "Foreign-born Population in the United States, 1850–2014," Pew Research Center.org, April 19, 2016, http://www.pewhispanic.org/2016/04/19/statistical-portrait-of-the-foreign-born-population-in-the-united-states-key-charts/#2013-fb-population.
3. United States Census Bureau, "U.S. and World Population Clock," https://www.census.gov/popclock/.
4. Brown and Stepler.

CHAPTER 1. PAINTERS

1. John Platt, "5 Things You Didn't Know About John James Audubon," mothernaturenetwork.com, April 26, 2011, http://www.mnn.com/earth-matters/wilderness-resources/stories/5-things-you-didnt-know-about-john-james-audubon.
2. The Art Story, "Joseph Stella: American Painter," http://www.theartstory.org/artist-stella-joseph.htm.
3. Danielle Peltakian, "Joseph Stella (1877–1946): American Futurist & Symbolist," SullivanGoss.com, http://www.sullivangoss.com/Joseph_Stella/.
4. Robert Lebel, "Marcel Duchamp," *Encyclopedia Britannica*, December 27, 2016, https://www.britannica.com/biography/Marcel-Duchamp.
5. Museum of Modern Art, "Dada: Discover How Dada Artists Used Chance, Collaboration, and Language as a Catalyst for Creativity," https://www.moma.org/learn/moma_learning/themes/dada/marcel-duchamp-and-the-readymade.

6. Dr. Lara Kuykendall, "Duchamp, The Bride Stripped Bare by Her Bachelors, Even (The Large Glass)," Khan Academy, https://www.khanacademy.org/humanities/art-1010/wwi-dada/dada1/a/duchamp-the-bride-stripped-bare-by-her-bachelors-even.
7. Karole P. B. Vail, *Peggy Guggenheim: A Celebration* (New York, NY: Guggenheim Museum, 1998), p. 43.
8. Vail, p. 47.
9. Jed Rasula, *Destruction Was My Beatrice* (New York, NY: Basic Books, 2015), p. XIII.
10. Vail, p. 52.
11. Art UK, "Max Ernst: 1891–1976," artuk.org, https://artuk.org/discover/artists/ernst-max-18911976.
12. Art UK, "Max Ernst: 1891–1976."
13. The Art Story, "Max Ernst: German Painter and Sculptor," http://www.theartstory.org/artist-ernst-max.htm.

CHAPTER 2. PHOTOGRAPHERS

1. "Nicéphore Niépce, Daguerre and the Physautotype," PhotoMuseum.org, http://www.photo-museum.org/niepce-nicephore-daguerre-physautotype/.
2. British Library, "Invention of Photography: 1830s," http://www.bl.uk/learning/timeline/item106980.html.
3. Rebecca Solnit, *River of Shadows: Eadweard Muybridge and the Technological Wild West* (New York, NY: Penguin, 2003), p. 7.
4. Ibid.
5. Edward Ball, *The Inventor and the Tycoon* (New York, NY: Doubleday, 2013), p. 181.
6. Biography.com, "Eadweard Muybridge," http://www.biography.com/people/eadweard-muybridge-9419513#synopsis.
7. Ball, p. 36.

8. Scholastic.com, "Interactive Tour of Ellis Island," http://teacher.scholastic.com/activities/immigration/tour/.

9. Ball, p. 242.

10. Biography.com, "Eadweard Muybridge."

11. Mitchell Leslie, "The Man Who Stopped Time," *Stanford*, https://alumni.stanford.edu/get/page/magazine/article/?article_id=39117.

12. *Encyclopedia Britannica*, "Eadweard Muybridge: British Photographer," https://www.britannica.com/biography/Eadweard-Muybridge.

13. Famous Photographers, "Elliott Erwitt," http://www.famousphotographers.net/elliott-erwitt.

14. Michael Kaplan, "Elliot Erwitt at Work," *American Photo*, May 1, 2014, http://www.americanphotomag.com/elliott-erwitt-work#page-7.

15. Magnum Photos, "Overview," https://www.magnumphotos.com/about-magnum/overview/.

16. Tiffany Hagler-Geard, "The Historic 'Napalm Girl' Pulitzer Image Marks Its 40th Anniversary," ABCNews.com, June 8, 2012, http://abcnews.go.com/blogs/headlines/2012/06/the-historic-napalm-girl-pulitzer-image-marks-its-40th-anniversary/.

CHAPTER 3. SCULPTORS

1. Ker Than, "Oldest North American Rock Art May Be 14,800 Years Old," *National Geographic,* August 15, 2013, http://news.nationalgeographic.com/news/2013/08/130815-lake-winnemucca-petroglyphs-ancient-rock-art-nevada/.

2. The Art Story, "Louise Bourgeois: French-American Sculptor," http://www.theartstory.org/artist-bourgeois-louise.htm.

3. *New Yorker*, "The Spider's Web," February 4, 2002, http://www.newyorker.com/magazine/2002/02/04/the-spiders-web.

4. Ibid.

5. Museum of Modern Art, "Louise Bourgeois: The Complete Prints & Books," https://www.moma.org/explore/collection/lb/about/biography.

6. *New Yorker,* "The Spider's Web."

7. Beth Gersh-Nesic, "Artists in 60 Seconds: Louise Bourgeois," arthistory.about.com, June 16, 2014, http://arthistory.about.com/od/namesbb/a/Louise-Bourgeois-biography.htm.

8. The Art Story, "Louise Bourgeois: French-American Sculptor."

9. Germaine Greer, "Louise Bourgeois's Greatest Creation Was the Contradictory Story of Her Life," *Guardian,* June 6, 2010, https://www.theguardian.com/artanddesign/2010/jun/06/louise-bourgeois.

10. BBC, "US Sculptor Louise Bourgeois Dies Aged 98," June 1, 2010, http://news.bbc.co.uk/2/hi/8714974.stm.

11. Lauren Palmer, "7 Quotes from Louise Bourgeois on Her Birthday," artnet.com, December 25, 2015, https://news.artnet.com/art-world/louise-bourgeois-quotes-on-her-birthday-390629.

12. Ibid.

13. "The Art Story, "Louise Bourgeois: French-American Sculptor."

14. Guggenheim Museum, "Eva Hesse: 1936-1970," https://www.guggenheim.org/artwork/artist/Eva-Hesse.

15. Kevin Madden, "Eva Hesse, Sol LeWitt, and Seventeen Magazine," utexas.edu, February 10, 2014, https://sites.utexas.edu/blanton/2014/02/eva-hesse-sol-lewitt-and-seventeen.html.

16. Tate, "Teacher and Group Leader's Kit: Eva Hesse: 13 November 02 – 9 March 03," http://www.tate.org.uk/download/file/fid/6384.

17. NYC Parks, "The Battery: The Immigrants," https://www.nycgovparks.org/parks/battery-park/monuments/765.

18. Eva Hesse Documentary, "About Hesse," https://www.evahessedoc.com/about-eva-hesse.

19. Ethan Gilsdorf, "The Dwarven Lord of Kickstarter," boingboing.net, July 31, 2015, http://boingboing.net/2015/07/31/the-dwarven-lord-of-kickstarte.html.

20. Willie Clark, "Meet the Man Who Raised Millions Crafting D&D Dungeons," motherboard.vice.com, September 4, 2016, https://motherboard.vice.com/en_us/article/meet-the-man-who-raised-millions-crafting-dd-dungeons.

21. Art in a Busy World (blog), "Irwin Greenberg (1922–2009)," September 25, 2010, http://artinabusyworld.blogspot.com/2010/09/irwin-greenberg-1922-2009.html.

22. The Long Shot (blog), "Just a Guy Who Played D&D," December 13, 2015, https://thelongshotist.com/tag/stefan-pokorny/.

CHAPTER 4. MIXED MEDIA ARTISTS

1. Tate, "Mixed Media," http://www.tate.org.uk/learn/online-resources/glossary/m/mixed-media.

2. Susan Hodara, "On the Glass House Pond, Yayoi Kusama's Clattering Polka Dots," *New York Times*, July 1, 2016, https://www.nytimes.com/2016/07/03/nyregion/on-the-glass-houses-pond-yayoi-kusamas-clattering-polka-dots.html.

3. "Yayoi Kusama: Look Now, See Forever," http://interactive.qag.qld.gov.au/looknowseeforever/timeline/.

4. Ibid.

5. Colin Schultz, "Nearly 6,000 Migrants Have Died Along the Mexico-U.S. Border Since 2000," smithsonianmag.com, October 1, 2014, http://www.smithsonianmag.com/smart-news/nearly-6000-migrants-have-died-along-mexico-us-border-2000-180952904/.

6. Rachel Cole, "Yayoi Kusama: Japanese Artist," *Encyclopedia Britannica*,https://www.britannica.com/biography/Yayoi-Kusama.

7. Artnet, "Yayoi Kusama (Japanese, born 1929)," http://www.artnet.com/artists/yayoi-kusama/biography.

8. David Pilling, "The World According to Yayoi Kusama," *Financial Times*, January 20, 2012, https://www.ft.com/content/52ab168a-4188-11e1-8c33-00144feab49a.

9. Miya Masaoka, "Unfinished Music," August 27, 1997, http://www.

miyamasaoka.com/interdisciplinary/writing/sfbg_yoko_ono. html.

10. The Art Story, "Yoko Ono: Japanese-American Conceptual and Performance Artist, and Musician," http://www.theartstory.org/ artist-ono-yoko.htm.

11. The Art Story, "Fluxus," http://www.theartstory.org/movement-fluxus.htm.

12. Molly Crane-Newman, "As Yoko Ono Celebrates Her U.S. Citizenship Anniversary, a Look at Other Celebs Who Immigrated to America," *Daily News*, March 24, 2016, http://www. nydailynews.com/entertainment/celebs-search-american-dream-article-1.2576561.

CHAPTER 5. COMIC BOOK ARTISTS

1. Calvin Reid, "North American Comics Market Reaches $1.03 Billion," *Publishers Weekly*, July 13, 2016, http://www. publishersweekly.com/pw/by-topic/industry-news/comics/ article/70897-north-american-comics-graphic-novel-market-reaches-1-03-billion.html.

2. Gerard Jones, *Men of Tomorrow: Geeks, Gangsters, and the Birth of the Comic Book* (NY: Basic Books, 2004), p. 67.

3. Jones, p. 69.

4. Deborah Friedell, "Kryptonomics: Why Superman's Creators Got a Raw Deal," *New Yorker*, June 24, 2016, http://www.newyorker.com/ magazine/2013/06/24/kryptonomics.

5. Ohio History Central, "Joe Shuster," http://www.ohiohistorycentral. org/w/Joe_Shuster.

6. Friedell, "Kryptonomics: Why Superman's Creators Got a Raw Deal."

7. Revolvy, "The Adventures of Superman (radio)," https://www. revolvy.com/main/index.php?s=The%20Adventures%20of%20 Superman%20(radio).

8. Sergioaragones.com, "About Sergio," http://sergioaragones.com/about-sergio/.

9. Reed Johnson, "Ojai Museum Fetes *Mad Magazines*' Sergio Aragonés," *Los Angeles Times*, August 9, 2009, http://www.latimes.com/entertainment/la-ca-aragones9-2009aug09-story.html.

10. R. C. Baker, "How Trump Magazine Sharply Satirized Americana," *Village Voice*, January 10, 2017, http://www.villagevoice.com/arts/how-trump-magazine-sharply-satirized-americana-9547251.

11. Reed Johnson, "Ojai Museum Fetes *Mad Magazines*' Sergio Aragonés."

12. Sergioaragones.com, "About Sergio," http://sergioaragones.com/about-sergio/.

13. *Encyclopedia Britannica*, "Winsor McCay: American Animator," https://www.britannica.com/biography/Winsor-McCay.

14. Ibid.

15. Encyclopedia.com, "Spiegelman, Art 1948," http://www.encyclopedia.com/people/history/historians-miscellaneous-biographies/art-spiegelman.

16. Jewish Virtual Library, "Spiegelman, Art 1948–," http://www.jewishvirtuallibrary.org/art-spiegelman

CHAPTER 6. FILM AND ANIMATION ARTISTS

1. Doug Chiang Studio, "Doug Chiang: Biography," http://www.dchiang.com/dchiang/aboutus.html.

2. College for Creative Studies, "Doug Chiang," https://www.collegeforcreativestudies.edu/Alumni/2822/Chiang/.

3. Azadeh Ansari and Joe Sutton, "Walt Disney '*Bambi*' Artist Dies at 106," CNN.com, December 30, 2016, http://www.cnn.com/2016/12/30/us/disney-bambi-artist-tyrus-wong-obituary/.

4. The Star, "*Star Wars* Artist Doug Chiang Talks About Designing a Galaxy Far Far Away for the Force Awakens," April 13, 2015, https://www.thestar.com/entertainment/movies/2015/04/13/star-

wars-artist-doug-chiang-talks-about-designing-a-galaxy-far-far-away-for-the-force-awakens.html.

5. Steve Tilley, "'*Star Wars*' Visual Director Doug Chiang Misses His Mentor George Lucas," *Toronto Sun*, April 8, 2015, http://www.torontosun.com/2015/04/08/star-wars-visual-director-doug-chiang-misses-his-mentor-george-lucas.

6. *Star Wars* Celebration, "Designing the Art of *Star Wars* with the Master: Doug Chiang," http://www.starwarscelebration.com/en/Sessions/28703/Designing-the-Art-of-Star-Wars-with-the-Master-Doug-Chiang.

7. Doug Chiang Studio, "Doug Chiang: Biography."

8. Serdar Yegulalp, "A Brief History of Anime," thoughtco.com, February 19, 2017, https://www.thoughtco.com/brief-history-of-anime-144979.

9. Jennie Wood, "Manga and Anime: The Japanese Invasion," infoplease.com, http://www.infoplease.com/entertainment/books/manga-anime.html.

10. Anime News Network, "America's 2009 Anime Market Pegged at US $2.741 Billion," April 15, 2011, http://www.animenewsnetwork.com/news/2011-04-15/america-2009-anime-market-pegged-at-us$2.741-billion.

11. YouTube, "Genndy's Scrapbook: The Story of Genndy Tartakovsky—Samurai Jack DVD Extras," https://www.youtube.com/watch?v=p5q6hwK13t4&t=5s.

12. Ibid.

13. Thelma Adams, "The Way We Live Now: Questions for Genndy Tartakovsky; The Big Draw," *New York Times*, August 19, 2001, http://www.nytimes.com/2001/08/19/magazine/the-way-we-live-now-questions-for-genndy-tartakovsky-the-big-draw.html.

CHAPTER 7. STREET ARTISTS

1. Nicholas Ganz, *Graffiti Women: Street Art from Five Continents* (New York, NY: Abrams, 2006), p. 72.
2. Danielle Rahm, "Banksy: The $20 Million Graffiti Artist Who Doesn't Want His Art to Be Worth Anything," Forbes.com, October, 22, 2013, http://www.forbes.com/sites/daniellerahm/2013/10/22/banksy-the-20-million-graffiti-artist-who-doesnt-want-his-art-to-be-worth-anything/#11f28e8e5f28.
3. N.I. Aya, "Lady Pink," widewalls.ch, http://www.widewalls.ch/artist/lady-pink/.
4. Eli Anapur, "The History of Train Graffiti," widewalls.ch, http://www.widewalls.ch/train-graffiti/.
5. N.I. Aya, "Lady Pink."
6. Ibid.
7. Nancy Ruhling, "Astoria Characters: The 'Pink' Painter," HuffingtonPost.com, March 4, 2013, http://www.huffingtonpost.com/nancy-ruhling/astoria-characters-lady-pink-graffiti_b_2129141.html.
8. Rogallery.com, "Lady Pink, Ecuadorian/American (1964–)," http://rogallery.com/Lady_Pink/lady_pink-biography.html.
9. Nancy Ruhling, "Astoria Characters: The 'Pink' Painter."
10. Biography.com, "Banksy Biography," http://www.biography.com/people/banksy-20883111#synopsis.
11. Jack Shepherd, "Banksy Identity: There's a Wild Theory the Graffiti Artist Is 3D of Massive Attack," *Independent*, September 2, 2016, http://www.*independent*.co.uk/arts-entertainment/art/news/banksy-identity-theres-a-wild-theory-the-graffiti-artist-is-3d-of-massive-attack-a7222326.html.
12. Allyssia Alleyne, "Welcome to Dismaland: Bansky's New Grotesque Art Theme Park," CNN.com, August 8, 2015, http://www.cnn.com/2015/08/20/arts/banksy-dismaland-art-exhibition/.

13. Artnet, "Mr. Brainwash," http://www.artnet.com/artists/mr-brainwash/biography.

14. Los Angeles Times, "Mr. Brainwash Was Always a Ham, High School Teacher Says," February 23, 2011, http://latimesblogs.latimes.com/movies/2011/02/mr-brainwash-was-always-a-ham-high-school-teacher-says-.html.

15. Alissa Walker, "Here's Why the Banksy Movie Is a Banksy Prank," FastCompany.com, April 15, 2010, https://www.fastcompany.com/1616365/heres-why-banksy-movie-banksy-prank.

16. Michelle Marie Robles Wallace, "Meet the Artists Using the US-Mexico Border as a Blank Canvas," Vice.com, June 29, 2016, https://www.vice.com/en_uk/article/the-artists-using-the-us-mexico-border-as-a-blank-canvas.

17. Border Artists, "La Frontera: Artists Along the U.S. Mexico Border," https://borderartists.com.

18. Cat Weaver, "Mr. Brainwash's Brain-dead Copyright Defense," Hyperallergic.com, May 3, 2013, http://hyperallergic.com/70326/mr-brainwashs-brain-dead-copyright-defense/.

GLOSSARY

Bering Strait Narrow passage that separates the tip of Siberia from Alaska and links the Arctic Ocean with the Bering Sea.

Creole Person born of European and Caribbean descent.

Dada Art movement of the early twentieth century that shunned traditionalism and produced works that were absurd or shocking.

emigrate To leave one's own country to move to another.

Fauvism Art movement of the early twentieth century that emphasized strong color over realistic representation.

Futurist Art movement of the early twentieth century that focused on industrialization, technology, and movement.

highbrow Refined or scholarly tastes.

Holocaust The systematic murder of six million Jews by German Nazis during World War II.

immigrate To come to a country from another one to live there permanently.

Impressionism Art movement of the nineteenth century depicting a feeling or experience rather than an accurate depiction.

inbetweener An artist who fills in the animation between key frames.

juxtapose To place close together to make a contrast.

napalm A flammable substance used in bombs and flamethrowers.

ornithologist A zoologist who studies birds.

parody An exaggerated imitation for comic effect.

petroglyph A rock carving, such as one made during prehistoric times.

psychoanalysis A system of therapy that treats the mind's conscious and unconscious thoughts.

readymade A type of artwork in which a common or mass-produced object is presented as art.

retrospective An art exhibit showing works done over a long period of time.

Surrealism Art movement of the twentieth century that often juxtaposed images or ideas for the viewer.

undocumented Not having the appropriate legal documents.

zoopraxiscope Device that uses a rotating disk so the viewer can see the images move rapidly in order, giving the impression of motion.

FURTHER READING

BOOKS

Alexander, Stuart, and Sean Corcoran. *Elliot Erwitt: Home Around the World*. New York, NY: Aperture, 2016.

Bouvier, Raphael. *Max Ernst: Retrospective*. Ostfildern, Germany: Hatje Cantz, 2013.

Chiang, Doug. *Mechanika, Revised and Updated: Creating the Art of Space, Aliens, Robots, and Sci-Fi*. Oakland, CA: Impact Publishers, 2015.

Lenburg, Jeff. *Genndy Tartakovsky: From Russia to Coming-of-Age Animator*. New York, NY: Chelsea House Publishing, 2012.

Ono, Yoko, and Julia Bryan-Wilson. *Yoko Ono: One Woman Show, 1960–1971*. New York, NY: The Museum of Modern Art, 2015.

Plain, Nancy. *The Strange Wilderness: The Life and Art of John James Audubon*. Lincoln, NE: University of Nebraska Press, 2015.

Ricca, Brad. *Super Boys: The Amazing Adventures of Jerry Siegel and Joe Shuster—The Creators of Superman*. New York, NY: St. Martin's Press, 2013.

Rosen, Barry, and Susan Fisher Sterling. *Eva Hesse 1965*. New Haven, CT: Yale University Press, 2013.

Spiegelman, Art. *The Complete Maus, 25th Anniversary Edition*. New York, NY: Pantheon, 1996.

Tapies, Xavier. *Where's Banksy?: Banksy's Greatest Works in Context*. Berkeley, CA: Ginko Press, Inc., 2016.

Tomkins, Calvin, and Marcel Duchamp. *Marcel Duchamp: The Afternoon Interviews*. New York, NY: Badlands Unlimited, 2013.

Wong, Tyrus, and Michael Labrie. *Water to Paper, Paint to Sky: The Art of Tyrus Wong*. New York, NY: Walt Disney Family Foundation Press, 2013.

WEBSITES

ArtsConnection

artsconnection.org/teen-programs

ArtsConnection works with schools to teach students about different types of art. Learn about the many programs it provides for teens, including tickets to exhibits and cultural events.

The Met

www.metmuseum.org/events/programs/teens

Founded in 1870, the Metropolitan Museum of Art has art from around the world, spanning five thousand years, for the public to enjoy. Learn about the summer programs, internships, and classes the museum offers for teens.

MoMa Learning

www.moma.org/learn/moma_learning/themes/migration-and-movement

MoMA Learning is a website of the Museum of Modern Art that focuses on the teaching and learning of modern and contemporary art. Learn more about Surrealism, Minimalism, and other styles of art.

National Conference of State Legislatures (NCSL)

www.ncsl.org/research/immigration/a-look-at-immigrant-youth-prospects-and-promisin.aspx

Formed in 1975, the NSCL is an organization that serves US lawmakers and other government workers. It includes information on the challenges immigrant youths have, such as not speaking English and struggles in school.

New York Foundation for the Arts

www.nyfa.org/Content/Show/Immigrant%20Artist%20Program%20 (IAP)

Established in 1971, the New York Foundation for the Arts is a nonprofit that helps artists during important times in their lives. Learn how the foundation has supported some of the nation's most famous artists.

NOLO

www.nolo.com/legal-encyclopedia/immigration-options-teenagers-without-lawful-status.html

NOLO offers a large library of legal information. Learn about the rights young people who are undocumented have in the United States.

US Department of Education

www2.ed.gov/about/overview/focus/immigration-resources.html

Run by the federal government, the US Department of Education provides a variety of information about immigrants, refugees, and other newcomers to the country. Learn more about their experiences.

INDEX

A

anime and manga, 79
Aragonés, Sergio, 66–67
    awards, 67
    birth, 66
    legacy, 67
    Mad Magazine, 66
art, history of, 6
    contributions, 9
    foreign-born artists, 8–9
Audubon, John James, 10–13
    birth, 10
    naturalist painter, 10
    death and legacy, 13, 15

B

Banksy, 88–89
border wall art, 92–93
Bourgeois, Louise, 38–44
    birth, 39
    death and legacy, 44
    difficult family life, 39, 42, 44
    feminist, 44
    sculptures, 39, 42
    spiders, 42

C

Chiang, Doug, 73–78
    birth, 73
    film production designer, 73
    legacy, 78
    Star Wars, 73, 75, 78
Cornell, Joseph, 20, 55
Cubism, 10, 17, 18

D

Dada, 10, 18, 24
Duchamp, Marcel, 17–20
    birth, 17
    death and legacy, 20
    painting, 17, 20
    readymade art, 17

E

Ernst, Max, 20–24
    birth, 20
    collage art, 22
    Dada and Surrealism, 24
    death and legacy, 24
Erwitt, Elliot, 33–36
    birth, 33
    black-and-white photography, 33
    legacy, 36
    Magnum Photos, 33
    photographed celebrities and dogs, 36

F

Fabara, Sandra (Lady Pink), 85–87
    birth, 85
    graffiti street artist, 85
    legacy, 87

social issues, 87

Wild Style, 85, 87

Fauvism, 17

Futurist, 13, 15, 17

G

graffiti, 83

history of, 83, 85

Guetta, Thierry (Mr. Brainwash), 89

birth, 89

controversy, 91, 93

legacy, 93

street artist, 89

Guggenheim, Peggy, 22–23, 24

H

Hesse, Eva, 44–48, 55

birth, 44

death and legacy, 48

found object sculptures, 44, 46

ill health, 48

I

Immigrants, The, 47

immigration artifacts exhibit, 54

Impressionism, 17

K

Kusama, Yayoi, 51–55

birth, 51

hallucinations, 51, 54

legacy, 55

mental hospital, 55

mixed media artist, 51

performance art, 55

L

Lennon, John, 58

death of, 59

marriage to Yoko Ono, 58

M

McCay, Winsor, 68

memes, 59

Minimalism, 44, 54

mixed media, 51

Muybridge, Eadweard, 26–31

birth, 26

created zoopraxiscope, 31

death and legacy, 31

head injury, 28–29

motion picture photography, 26, 29

murder charge, 29

photographed horses, 29, 31

N

National Audubon Society, 13

O

Ono, Yoko, 55–61

birth, 55, 57

death of Lennon, 59, 61

Fluxus, 58

legacy, 61

marriages, 55, 58

mixed media artist, 55
performance art, 55, 58, 61

P

photographs of US immigrants, 28
photography, 25–26
Pokorny, Stefan, 48–50
  birth, 38
  Dungeons and Dragons, 48, 50
  Dwarven Forge, 48, 50
  legacy, 50
  sculptures, 48
Pop Art, 54, 89

S

Schuster, Joe, 62–65
  birth, 63
  co-creator of Superman, 62, 64
  death and legacy, 64, 65
sculpture, 37
Siegel, Jerry, 62, 64
  co-creator of Superman, 64
  death, 64–65
Spiegelman, Art, 68–72
  birth, 68–69, 71
  comic book artist, 68
  Holocaust, 68–69
  legacy, 72
  Maus, 68, 72
  Pulitzer Prize, 72
  Raw, 68
Statue of Liberty, 40

Stella, Joseph, 13–17
  birth, 13
  death and legacy, 15, 17
  Futurist painter, 13, 15
  magazine illustrator, 13
Surrealism, 10, 18, 24

T

Tartakovsky, Genndy, 78–82
  animator, 78
  birth, 78–79
  cartoon shows, 80–81
  legacy, 82
  Star Wars: Clone Wars, 81–82
  The Powerpuff Girls, 81

U

undocumented immigrant superheroes, 65
Undocumented Migration Project, 54
US immigrants, history of, 6, 8–9
Ut, Nick, 34

W

war and immigration, 18
Wong, Tyrus, 76
  Bambi, 76

Z

zoopraxiscope, 31

ADAM FURGANG

Adam Furgang is a writer and artist. He studied art at the High School of Art and Design in New York City and illustration at the University of the Arts in Philadelphia. Before becoming a writer, Adam worked as a graphic designer, web designer, photographer, and fine artist. He continues to produce art and take pictures frequently.

Adam's current writing credits include more than twenty nonfiction books in the middle school library market about topics such as art, photography, video games, pop culture, and science. He also has two novels published, *Braxton Woods Mystique* (2016) and *Monster Runners* (2017), from Ravenswood Publishing.

Three of Adam's grandparents were immigrants, coming to the United States from Poland and Russia, with a step-grandfather coming from China. Adam grew up in an ethnically diverse family and has a rich understanding and respect for peoples and cultures from around the world.